D1285132

STANDARD CITATION FORMS
FOR PUBLISHED BIBLIOGRAPHIES AND CATALOGS USED IN
RARE BOOK CATALOGING

-First edition-

Prepared by Peter VanWingen and Stephen Paul Davis
Library of Congress

Authorized for use in rare book cataloging by the
Standards Committee of the Rare Books and Manuscripts Section,
Association of College and Research Libraries,
American Library Association.

Library of Congress   Washington   1982

The cover illustration is a woodcut from the Nuremburg Chronicle (1493)
showing the first paper mill in Germany, built in 1390 by Ulman Stromer.

LIBRARY OF CONGRESS CATALOGING IN PUBLICATION DATA

VanWingen, Peter M.
  Standard citation forms for published bibliographies and catalogs used
in rare book cataloging.

  "Authorized for use in rare book cataloging by the Standards Committee
of the Rare Books and Manuscripts Section, Association of College and
Research Libraries, American Library Association."
  Includes index.

  1. Cataloging of rare books. 2. Bibliographical citations. 3. Bib-
liography--Bibliography--Rare books. 4. Rare books--Bibliography. I.
Davis, Stephen Paul. II. Library of Congress. III. Association of College and Research Libraries. Rare Books and Manuscripts Section. Standards Committee. IV. Title.

Z695.74.V36   025.3'416   82-600105
ISBN 0-8444-0395-4 (pbk.)   AACR2

Available from the Cataloging Distribution Service
Library of Congress, Washington, D.C. 20541

Introduction

This list is an attempt to draw together and establish citation forms for those works that are helpful in verifying, identifying, and describing items held in rare book and special collections. It is not a fixed canon of recommended bibliographic sources nor is it a bibliography of bibliographies: its sole purpose is to establish and record standardized citation forms.

Its use is, of course, optional, though it is recommended by the Standards Committee of the Rare Books and Manuscripts Section of the American Library Association, especially for those libraries using automated cataloging and retrieval systems. The citation forms suggested here may be used whenever the corresponding bibliographies or catalogs are cited in the note area of the bibliographic record, either in a general note or as a "References" note. (For description of the use of references to published descriptions in the note area of library catalog records see Anglo-American Cataloguing Rules. 2nd ed. Chicago: American Library Association, 1978, rules 1.7., ff., esp. 1.7B15; and Bibliographic Description of Rare Books. Washington: Library of Congress, 1981, rule 7, ff., esp. 7C14.) While we expect that these citation forms will be used chiefly in library cataloging, we hope that others creating bibliographic descriptions will also find them helpful and use them whenever practicable.

This list is based on one originally prepared for the Ad Hoc Committee on Standards for Rare Book Cataloguing in Machine-Readable Form of the Independent Research Libraries Association, which appeared in that Committee's Proposals for Establishing Standards for the Cataloguing of Rare Books and Specialized Research Materials in Machine Readable Form: Interim Draft (Sept. 1979). In its present form it reflects bibliographies found most useful in describing the holdings of the Rare Book and Special Collections Division of the Library of Congress as well as those suggested by members of the RBMS Standards Committee, the American Antiquarian Society, and others who commented on the Ad Hoc Committee's Interim Draft. Other institutions will be able to identify bibliographic sources that they need to cite in cataloging their own collections, and we will rely on these institutions to bring to our attention additional candidates for inclusion as set out in section II of the Working Principles.

The entries have been prepared chiefly from Library of Congress catalog records for the items or, where no LC record exists, from the National Union Catalog entry; in most cases, the books themselves have not been re-examined. Because of this modus operandi, it is possible that an occasional cataloging error or inaccuracy has been unwittingly incorporated. We will do our best to correct such problems as they come to light.

It is our hope that this list will benefit catalog users in several ways: it will provide a consistent citation method for references to published descriptions; it will offer a key by which unfamiliar reference citations may be identified; and it will make possible the efficient computer-based retrieval of specific works by means of unique citation numbers, or of sets of works by virtue of their inclusion in a particular bibliography or catalog.

An argument might be made for restricting the scope of the list to those bibliographies in which the individual descriptions are numbered, on the ground that only these provide the unique access points useful for computer-based retrieval. We have proceeded on the theory, however, that there may well be value in citing unnumbered bibliographies in a standard way, with or without page numbers, for the possible subject, chronological, or other access that they could provide in an automated system. Hence both numbered and un-numbered bibliographies have been included here.

For a future edition, we are considering adding a subject index, which might make the list more useful for identifying less well-known bibliographies. Before undertaking this, however, we would be interested in comments on this proposal from users of the list.

Please address all comments and requests for additions, revisions, or corrections, along with appropriate documentation (cf. Working Principles, section II.A) to: Peter VanWingen, Rare Book and Special Collections Division, Library of Congress, Washington, D.C. 20540.

Peter VanWingen
Stephen Paul Davis

Working Principles

I. Scope.

The following list includes bibliographies that are useful in verifying, identifying, or describing items held in rare book or special collections and that have been or are likely to be cited in machine-readable cataloging records. Bibliographies of or about individuals, printers, publishers, or jurisdictions below the national level are largely excluded from this list, both because of the great number of such publications and because the application of the formula set out in section IV.F below will in most cases result in a consistent citation form.

II. Maintenance.

A. For sources that are not on this list, the working principles should be applied to create a standard citation form. If the citation is to be used in a "References" note in a MARC record, and is within the scope of the list, the cataloging institution is urged to request that the editor add the source.

The editor will add a bibliography or catalog that is within the scope of this list and assign it a citation form whenever requested to do so by the RBMS Standards Committee or by any institution engaged in the processing of rare materials. To be considered, such a request should be made in writing and should include:

1) a full bibliographical description;

2) a suggested citation form;

3) an indication that the bibliography or catalog has been, or will be, cited in a "References" note in a MARC cataloging record by the requesting library. A print-out or photocopy of the MARC record in which the bibliography has been cited should be included, if feasible.

B. The editor may also add a bibliography or catalog to the list in advance of any formal request, if, in his judgment, it is likely to be cited in a MARC record.

C. In general, only the most recent edition of a bibliography that has appeared in more than one edition should be included on the list, unless:

1) the new edition is a multivolume work that is not yet complete;

2) the new edition does not follow the same numbering scheme as the previous edition;

3) the new edition omits still valid information present in the earlier edition.

In any of the above cases, earlier editions will be retained in the list so long as they are useful.

D. The editor will prepare updates to the list at appropriate intervals and have them published in the library press. Upon the advice of the Standards Committee, the editor will prepare a new edition for publication.

III. The Bibliographic Entry.

A. Construction of the basic entry. The basic entry for a bibliography or catalog generally follows the style recommended by the University of Chicago Press in its Manual of Style for Authors, Editors, and Copywriters (12th ed., rev. Chicago: University of Chicago Press, 1969). However, works are always entered under the main entry heading as established by the Library of Congress, if this can be determined. The entire LC heading (with full forenames, etc.) is used, omitting only such information as birthdates and nonessential parenthetical information. Normal bracketing conventions are used as prescribed in the Manual of Style; ISBD punctuation is not used.

B. AACR 2. In general, forms of headings in the entries are based on Library of Congress headings that predate AACR 2. These will not ordinarily be changed in future editions of the list. However, if a work is later added that the Library of Congress has entered under a revised AACR 2 heading, and there are other works on the list entered under a pre-AACR 2 form of the same heading, all affected headings in the list will be changed to the AACR 2 form at the same time. An already-established citation form will not ordinarily be modified, however.

C. Supplements. If a supplement to or continuation of another bibliography continues the numbering of the main work, or is physically integral with the main work, or is not well-known as a separate work, it is included in the list as a subordinate entry under the main work. Otherwise, a separate entry is made.

As an exception, if a supplement continuing the numbering of the main work has become well-known under its own author or title, a separate entry and citation form is established.

For the form of citation for supplements, see section IV.E below.

D. Reprints. When a bibliography has also been published in a reprint edition, information about the reprint may be added after the information about the original. In the present edition of this list, reprint information has been recorded when readily available; no special research has been undertaken to identify additional reprints. Note that in many cases, reprint editions also contain additions and corrections or supplements to the original. No attempt has been made to note the presence or absence of such additional material in reprints. A qualifier should always be added to the basic citation form when citing such supplementary material even if it has been reprinted in a single volume with the original text (Cf. section IV.E below).

E. Cross references. Cross references have been sparingly added to the list in a few cases in which a bibliography is known under a name or title other than that chosen as the LC main entry or the citation form.

IV. Construction of the Citation Form.

A. Works Entered Under a Personal Name.

1. If a work is entered under a personal name, generally give the citation in the following pattern:

>   Surname, Forename Initial(s). Keyword(s) of title

Leave two spaces after the period separating the forename initials from the title word(s). Do not leave any spaces between forename initials.

Use forename initials in the citation form corresponding to the forenames in the established Library of Congress heading.

If there are two joint authors, construct the author portion of the citation form by using surnames only, joined by an ampersand.

>   Houzeau & Lancaster. Astronomie (1964 ed.)

If there are three or more joint authors, use the surname and forename initials of the first author only for the author portion of the author/title citation. If this is not appropriate, use some other element as the citation form (e.g., title alone, corporate name/title).

In formulating the title portion of the author/title citation, select the first word or words from the title proper or other keyword(s) if these better characterize the work. Omit any initial articles. Change ampersands appearing in the title portion of the citation to the word "and" in the appropriate language.

2. If a work has become widely known by the author's last name, that name alone may constitute the citation form. This applies also to works with joint authors.

>   Evans
> not   Evans, C. Amer. bibl.
>
>   Shipton & Mooney
> not   Shipton & Mooney. Short-title Evans

3. If a work has become widely known by its title it may be cited by title keyword(s) alone, even though it is entered under a personal name.

4. If an edition of a work subsequent to the first has been prepared or revised by someone other than the original author and the work has become known by both names, it may be cited by hyphenating the names. The work's title may either be added or omitted, according to how it is generally cited.

> work: Backer, Augustine de. Bibliothèque de la Compagnie de
>   Jesus. Nouv. éd. par Carlos Sommervogel. Bruxelles:
>   O. Schepens; Paris: A. Picard, 1890-1932.
>
> citation: Backer-Sommervogel

B. <u>Works Entered Under a Corporate Name.</u>

1. If a work is entered under a corporate name by the Library of Congress, generally use that name as the first element of the citation form. If the corporate name is hierarchical in its cataloging form, it may be cited in a non-hierarchical fashion with as much abridgement as is feasible.

>   entry: British Museum. Dept. of Printed Books.
>   use: BM

2. If a work entered under a corporate name under current or previous cataloging rules has become widely known either by its title or by the name of its editor, either of these elements may be used for the citation form in lieu of the corporate name.

>   work: United States. Library of Congress. Map Division. <u>A list of</u>
>   <u>geographical atlases in the Library of Congress, with bib-</u>
>   <u>liographical notes.</u> Vols. 1-4 comp. under the direction of
>   P.L. Phillips. [etc.]
>
>   citation: Phillips

3. In formulating the title portion of a corporate name/title citation, select the first word or words from the title proper or other keyword(s) if these better characterize the work. Omit any initial articles. Change ampersands appearing in the title portion to the word "and" in the appropriate language.

C. <u>Works Entered Under Title.</u>

1. If a work is entered under title by the Library of Congress, generally use keywords from the title as the citation form.

In formulating a title-only citation form, select the first word or words from the title proper or other keyword(s) if these better characterize the work. Omit any initial articles. Change an ampersand to the word "and" in the appropriate language.

2. If a work entered under title is generally cited by a personal author or editor or corporate body, the person or body may be used as the first element of the citation form.

D. <u>Works in Multiple Editions.</u> When assigning a citation form to an edition other than the first, if the citation form would be the same as that for the first edition, add in parentheses an abbreviated version of the edition statement. If the edition statement is not distinctive or if there is no edition statement, use the date of publication in its place (e.g., 1924 ed.). Generally use the language of the title and AACR 2 abbreviations when feasible in formulating this qualification. In exceptional cases, when a particular edition of a work is widely cited without reference to its edition, the edition qualification may be omitted from the citation form.

>   STC
>   STC (2nd ed.)

```
          Adams, R.F.  Six-guns (1969 ed.)
not       Adams, R.F.  Six-guns (new ed.)

          Brunet
not       Brunet (5. éd.)
```

E. Supplements. If a supplement is listed under the main work, always add the qualifier "suppl." (or another appropriate term or abbreviation) in parentheses to the citation form for the main work when citing the supplement, even if the numbering is continuous with that of the main work. Note that the citation forms for supplements have generally not been given explicitly in this list.

```
          Goff (suppl.)
          BM (1956-65)
```

If a supplement has a separate entry in the list, the general principles for establishing a citation form are applied. If the citation form for the supplement would be the same as or similar to that of the main work, the qualification "suppl." or another appropriate term may be added to the citation form for the main work in parentheses.

F. Categories of Bibliographies Excluded From the List. Bibliographies of or about individuals, printers, publishers, and jurisdictions below the national level are generally excluded from this list. However, these may ordinarily be cited according to the following formula:

```
    Compiler's surname, forename initial(s).  Name (of individual,
        printer, publisher, or jurisdiction)
```

```
          Purdy, R.L.  Hardy
          Miller, W.C.  Franklin
          Voet, L.  Plantin Press
          McCorison, M.A.  Vermont
```

For the author portion of the citation, follow the guidelines in IV.A-B above; if the work is entered under title, follow the instructions in IV.C above.

For bibliographies of or about a person, generally use the surname only of the subject as the title element of the citation. If the surname is not sufficient to distinguish the work from other works by the same author, additional names or title words may be added.

```
          Holmes, T.J.  Increase Mather
          Holmes, T.J.  Cotton Mather
          Holmes, T.J.  Minor Mathers
```

G. Abbreviations. Use standard abbreviations in citations, including--though not limited to--those listed in AACR 2, Appendix B.13, e.g.

```
Amer.  = America(n)
bib.   = bibliography, (bibliographie, etc.); bibliothèque
           (biblioteca, etc.)
Brit.  = British
cat.   = catalog(ue)
cats.  = catalog(ue)s
cent.  = century
coll.  = collection
Engl.  = English
incun. = incunabula, incunables
Jh.    = Jahrhundert(s)
Kat.   = Katalog
lib.   = library
libs.  = libraries
lit.   = literature (Literatur)
litt.  = littérature
nat.   = national(e)
rép.   = répertoire
s.     = siècle(s)
suppl. = supplement
univ.  = university (université, etc.)
```

V. Numeration.

When a bibliography or catalog is numbered, give the number exactly as it appears in the source. Add other information when needed for clarification.

```
        Evans 2046
but     Wing A12
        (Note: the "A" does not appear in the source)
```

For short, standard citations, separate the citation form from the number by one space.

```
        Goff D-143
        STC (2nd ed.) 18772.5
```

Whenever both author and title are cited and whenever title only (unless abbreviated) is cited, use a comma-space before the number to help clarify the phrase.

```
        Church, E.D.  Engl. lit., 319
        Artist and the book, 247
but     BAL 7242
```

When an unnumbered bibliography is cited, specific page numbers or other locational information may be given if desired. A comma-space should be used before a page or volume and page citation, and between a volume number and a page number. Volume numbers are generally given in upper case roman numerals. Beyond this, however, no high degree of consistency is necessary.

> BM 15th cent., VI, p. 53 (IB.52846)
> BM STC Italian, p. 271
> Lowndes, p. 809

VI. MARC Application.

The citation forms recommended in this list should be used whenever the corresponding bibliographies or catalogs are cited in a MARC bibliographic record, whether in a general note (500 field) or as a "References" note (510 field). These notes are described in AACR 2 rule 1.7B1 and following.

The "References" note should be a simple citation of the location of a description in a catalog or bibliography; it should not include other information. Additional information about the citation may be given in a general note. It is suggested that those titles which might be useful for retrieval always be cited in a "References" note, even in cases in which this would involve repetition of information already given in a general note:

> General note: Evans calls this the 2nd ed.
> "References" note: Evans 14023

Library of Congress MARC records will carry each "References" note in a separate 510 field without any ending punctuation. When printed cards or bibliographies are created from MARC records, the print constant "References:" will be generated ahead of the first occurrence of a 510 field. All 510 fields will be combined into a single paragraph; a semicolon will appear after each citation except the last, which will end in a period.

For details about the structure and use of fields 500 and 510, see <u>MARC Formats for Bibliographic Data</u> (Washington, D.C.: Automated Systems Office, Library of Congress, 1980-).

STANDARD CITATION FORMS

Abbey, John Roland. Life in England in aquatint and lithography, 1770-1860: architecture, drawing books, art collections, magazines, navy and army, panoramas, etc., from the library of J.R. Abbey: a bibliographical catalogue. London: Priv. print. at the Curwen Press, 1953. Reprint. Folkestone: Dawsons of Pall Mall, 1972.

CITE AS: Abbey, J.R. Life

Abbey, John Roland. Scenery of Great Britain and Ireland in aquatint and lithography, 1770-1860, from the library of J.R. Abbey: a bibliographical catalogue. London: Priv. print. at the Curwen Press, 1952. Reprint. Folkestone: Dawsons of Pall Mall, 1972.

CITE AS: Abbey, J.R. Scenery

Abbey, John Roland. Travel in aquatint and lithography, 1770-1860, from the library of J.R. Abbey: a bibliographical catalogue. London: Priv. print. at the Curwen Press, 1956-57. Reprint. Folkestone: Dawsons of Pall Mall, 1972.

CITE AS: Abbey, J.R. Travel

Adams, Herbert Mayow. Catalogue of books printed on the continent of Europe, 1501-1600, in Cambridge libraries. London: Cambridge University Press, 1967.

CITE AS: Adams

Adams, Ramon Frederick. Six-guns and saddle leather: a bibliography of books and pamphlets on western outlaws and gunmen. New ed., rev. and greatly enl. Norman: University of Oklahoma Press, 1969.

CITE AS: Adams, R.F. Six-guns (1969 ed.)

Adams, Thomas Randolph. The American controversy: a bibliographical study of the British pamphlets about the American disputes, 1764-1783. Providence: Brown University Press; New York: Bibliographical Society, 1980.

CITE AS: Adams, T.R. Brit. pamphlets

Adams, Thomas Randolph. American independence, the growth of an idea: a bibliographical study of the American political pamphlets printed between 1764 and 1776 dealing with the dispute between Great Britain and her colonies. Providence: Brown University Press, 1965.

CITE AS: Adams, T.R. Amer. pamphlets

Adomeit, Ruth E. Three centuries of thumb Bibles: a checklist. New York: Garland, 1980.

   CITE AS: Adomeit, R.E. Thumb Bibles

Aldis, Harry Gidney. A list of books printed in Scotland before 1700. Edinburgh: Edinburgh Bibliographical Society, 1904. Reprints. Edinburgh: National Library of Scotland, 1970. New York: B. Franklin, 1970.

   CITE AS: Aldis, H.G. Scotland

Allison, Antony Francis, and Rogers, David Morrison. A catalogue of Catholic books in English printed abroad or secretly in England, 1558-1640. Bognor Regis: Arundel Press, 1956. Reprint. London: W. Dawson, 1964.

   CITE AS: Allison & Rogers. Catholic books

Alston, R.C. A bibliography of the English language from the invention of printing to the year 1800: a systematic record of writings on English, and on other languages in English, based on the collections of the principal libraries of the world. Leeds, Eng.: Printed for the author by E.J. Arnold, 1965-72.

   CITE AS: Alston, R.C. Engl. language

American Antiquarian Society, Worcester, Mass. Library. A dictionary catalog of American books pertaining to the 17th through 19th centuries. Westport, Conn.: Greenwood Pub. Corp., 1971.

   CITE AS: AAS dictionary cat.

American Institute of Electrical Engineers. Library. Catalogue of the Wheeler gift of books, pamphlets, and periodicals in the library of the American Institute of Electrical Engineers. Ed. by William D. Weaver. New York: American Institute of Electrical Engineers, 1909.

   CITE AS: Wheeler gift

Anker, Jean. Bird books and bird art. Copenhagen: Levin & Munksgaard, 1938. Reprint. New York: Arno Press, 1974.

   CITE AS: Anker, J. Bird books

Arents, George. Tobacco: a catalogue .... SEE: New York (City). Public Library. Arents Tobacco Collection.

Arents, George. Tobacco, its history illustrated by the books, manuscripts, and engravings in the library of George Arents, Jr., together with an introductory essay, a glossary, and bibliographic notes by Jerome E. Brooks. New York: Rosenbach Co., 1937-52.

   CITE AS: Arents, G. Tobacco

Arnott, James Fullarton, and Robinson, John William. English theatrical literature, 1559-1900: a bibliography, incorporating Robert W. Lowe's "A bibliographical account of English theatrical literature" published in 1888. London: Society for Theatre Research, 1970.

   CITE AS: Arnott, J.F. Engl. theatrical lit.

The Ashley library .... **SEE:** Wise, Thomas James.

Ayer, Edward E. Catalogue of the Edward E. Ayer Ornithological Library. **SEE:** Field Museum of Natural History, Chicago.

Ayer, Edward E. Narratives of captivity .... **SEE:** Newberry Library, Chicago. Edward E. Ayer Collection.

Backer, Augustine de. Bibliothèque de la Compagnie de Jesus. Nouv. éd. par Carlos Sommervogel. Bruxelles: O. Schepens; Paris: A. Picard, 1890-1932. ----- ----- Corrections et additions. Par Ernest-M. Rivière. Toulouse: Rivière, 1911-17.

   CITE AS: Backer-Sommervogel

Bainton, A.J.C. Comedias sueltas in Cambridge University Library. **SEE:** Cambridge. University. Library.

Barbier, Antoine Alexandre. Dictionnaire des ouvrages anonymes. 3. éd., rev. et augm. Paris: P. Daffis, 1872-79. Reprint. Paris: G.P. Maisonneuve & Larose, 1964.

   CITE AS: Barbier, A.A. Ouvrages anonymes

Baudrier, Henri Louis. Bibliographie lyonnaise: recherches sur les imprimeurs, libraires, relieurs et fondeurs de lettres de Lyon au XVIe siècle. Publiées et continuées par J. Baudrier. Lyon: Librairie ancienne d'Auguste Brun, 1895-1921. ----- Table. Par George Tricou. Genève: E. Droz, 1950-52.

   CITE AS: Baudrier, H.L. Bib. lyonnaise

Beale, Joseph Henry. A bibliography of early English law books. Cambridge:
Harvard University Press, 1926.
----- ----- A supplement. 1943.

   CITE AS: Beale, J.H. Engl. law

Berlin. Kunstbibliothek. Katalog der Lipperheideschen Kostümbibliothek.
Neubearbeitet von Eva Nienholdt und Gretel Wagner-Neumann. 2. völlig
neubearb. u. verm. Aufl. Berlin: Mann, 1965.

   CITE AS: Lipperheidesche Kostümbibliothek (2. Aufl.)

Berlin. Staatliche Kunstbibliothek. Katalog der Ornamentstichsammlung der
Staatlichen Kunstbibliothek, Berlin. Berlin: Verlag für Kunstwissenschaft, 1939.

   CITE AS: Berlin. Ornamentstichsammlung

Bersano Begey, Marina. Le cinquecentine piemontesi. Torino: Tipografia
torinese editrice, 1961-66.

   CITE AS: Bersano Begey, M. Cinquecentine piemontesi

Besançon, France. Bibliothèque municipale. Catalogue des incunables de la
bibliothèque publique de Besançon. Par Auguste Castan. Besançon: J.
Dodivers, 1893.

   CITE AS: Besançon. Incun.

Besterman, Theodore. Old art books. London: Maggs Bros. Ltd., 1975.

   CITE AS: Besterman, T. Art books

Bibliographie der deutschen Drucke des XVI. Jahrhunderts. Bad Bocklet: W.
Krieg, 1960-

   CITE AS: Deutsche Drucke des 16. Jh.

Bibliotheca Belgica: bibliographie générale des Pays-Bas. Fondée par Ferd.
van der Haeghen et publiée sous sa direction. Gand: Vanderpoorten; La
Haye: M. Nijhoff, 1880-1923.

   CITE AS: Bib. Belgica

Bibliotheca Lindesiana ... **SEE:** Crawford, J.L.L.

Bigmore, Edward Clements, and Wyman, C.W.H., comps. A bibliography of
     printing, with notes and illustrations. London: B. Quaritch, 1880-86.
     Reprints. New York: P.C. Duschnes, 1945. London: Holland Press; Newark,
     Del.: Oak Knoll Books, 1978.

     CITE AS: Bigmore & Wyman

Bishop, William Warner. A checklist of American copies of "Short-title cata-
     logue" books. 2nd ed. Ann Arbor: University of Michigan Press, 1950.
     Reprint. New York: Greenwood Press, 1968.

     CITE AS: Bishop, W.W. Checklist (2nd ed.)

Bitting, Katherine Golden. Gastronomic bibliography. San Francisco, 1939.
     Reprint. Ann Arbor, Mich.: Gryphon Books, 1971.

     CITE AS: Bitting, K.G. Gastronomic bib.

Blanck, Jacob Nathaniel. Bibliography of American literature. Comp. for the
     Bibliographical Society of America. New Haven: Yale University Press,
     1955-

     CITE AS: BAL

Block, Andrew. The English novel, 1740-1850: a catalogue including prose
     romances, short stories, and translations of foreign fiction. London:
     Grafton & Co., 1939. Reprints. London: Dawsons of Pall Mall; Dobbs
     Ferry, N.Y.: Oceana, 1967. Westport, Conn.: Greenwood, 1981.

     CITE AS: Block, A. Engl. novel

Bohatta, Hanns. Bibliographie der Livres d'Heures (Horae B.M.V.): Officia,
     Hortuli Animae, Coronae B.M.V., Rosaria und Cursus B.M.V. des XV. und
     XVI. Jahrhunderts. 2. verm. Aufl. Wien: Gilhofer & Ranschburg, 1924.

     CITE AS: Bohatta, H. Livres d'Heures (2. Aufl.)

Bohonos, Maria, and Szandorowska, Elisa. Incunabula quae in bibliothecis Po-
     loniae asservantur. Wratislaviae: Ex Officina Instituti Ossoliniani,
     1970.

     CITE AS: IBP

Bond, Richmond Pugh, and Bond, Marjorie N. The Tatler and the Spectator and the development of the early periodic press in England: a checklist of the collection of Richmond P. Bond and Marjorie N. Bond. Chapel Hill, N.C., 1965.

CITE AS: Bond & Bond. Tatler

Borchling, Conrad, and Claussen, Bruno. Niederdeutsche Bibliographie: Gesamtverzeichnis der niederdeutschen Drucke bis zum Jahre 1800. Neumunster: K. Wachholtz Verlag, 1931-36.

CITE AS: Borchling & Claussen

Bosanquet, Eustace Fulcrand. English printed almanacks and prognostications: a bibliographical history to the year 1600. London: Printed for the Bibliographical Society at the Chiswick Press, 1917.
----- ----- Corrigenda and addenda. 1928.

CITE AS: Bosanquet, E.F. Almanacks

Boston. Museum of Fine Arts. The artist & the book, 1860-1960, in Western Europe and the United States. Boston: Museum of Fine Arts; Cambridge, Mass.: Harvard College Library, Dept. of Printing and Graphic Arts, 1961.

CITE AS: Artist and the book

Boyer, Mildred. The Texas collection of comedias sueltas: a descriptive bibliography. Boston: G.K. Hall, 1978.

CITE AS: Boyer, M. Texas coll. of sueltas

Brigham, Clarence Saunders. History and bibliography of American newspapers, 1690-1820. Worcester, Mass.: American Antiquarian Society, 1947. Reprint. Westport, Conn.: Greenwood Press, 1976.
----- ----- Additions and corrections. 1961.

CITE AS: Brigham, C.S. Amer. newspapers

Brinley, George. Catalogue of the American library of the late Mr. George Brinley, of Hartford, Conn. Hartford: Press of the Case, Lockwood & Brainard Co., 1878-93. Reprint. New York: AMS Press, 1968.

CITE AS: Brinley, G. Cat.

Bristol, Roger Pattrell. Supplement to Charles Evans' American bibliography. Charlottesville: Published for the Bibliographical Society of America and the Bibliographical Society of the University of Virginia [by] University Press of Virginia, 1970.

    CITE AS: Bristol

British and Foreign Bible Society. Library. Historical catalogue of the printed editions of Holy Scripture in the Library of the British and Foreign Bible Society. Comp. by T.H. Darlow and H.F. Moule. London: The Bible House, 1903-11.

    CITE AS: Darlow & Moule
    (Note: Herbert's revision is entered separately in this list.)

British Library. The British Library general catalogue of printed books to 1975. London: C. Bingley; London and New York: K.G. Saur, 1979-

    CITE AS: BLC

British Museum. Dept. of Printed Books. Catalogue of books printed in the XVth century now in the British Museum. London: Printed by order of the Trustees, 1908-71.

    CITE AS: BM 15th cent.

British Museum. Dept. of Printed Books. General catalogue of printed books to 1955. Photolithographic ed. London: Trustees of the British Museum, 1959-66.
----- ----- Ten-year supplement, 1956-1965. 1968.
----- ----- Five-year supplement, 1966-1970. 1971-72.

    CITE AS: BM
           BM (1956-65)
           BM (1966-70)

British Museum. Dept. of Printed Books. General catalogue of printed books to 1955. Compact ed. New York: Readex Microprint Corp., 1967-

    CITE AS: BM (compact ed.)

British Museum. Dept. of Printed Books. Short-title catalogue of books printed in France and of French books printed in other countries from 1470-1600 now in the British Museum. London: Printed by order of the Trustees, 1924. Reprint. London: British Museum, 1966.

    CITE AS: BM STC French, 1470-1600

British Museum. Dept. of Printed Books. <u>Short-title catalogue of books printed in Italy and of Italian books printed in other countries from 1465 to 1600 now in the British Museum.</u> London: Trustees of the British Museum, 1958.

    CITE AS: BM STC Italian, 1465-1600

British Museum. Dept. of Printed Books. <u>Short-title catalogue of books printed in Spain and of Spanish books printed elsewhere in Europe before 1601 now in the British Museum.</u> London: Printed by order of the Trustees, 1921.

    CITE AS: BM STC Spanish, pre-1601

British Museum. Dept. of Printed Books. <u>Short-title catalogue of books printed in the German-speaking countries and German books printed in other countries from 1455 to 1600 now in the British Museum.</u> London: Trustees of the British Museum, 1962.

    CITE AS: BM STC German, 1455-1600

British Museum. Dept. of Printed Books. <u>Short-title catalogue of books printed in the Netherlands and Belgium and of Dutch and Flemish books printed in other countries from 1470 to 1600 now in the British Museum.</u> London: Trustees of the British Museum, 1965.

    CITE AS: BM STC Dutch and Flemish, 1470-1600

British Museum. Dept. of Printed Books. <u>A short title catalogue of French books, 1601-1700 ...</u> **SEE:** Goldsmith, Valentine Fernande

British Museum. Dept. of Printed Books. <u>A short title catalogue of Spanish and Portuguese books, 1601-1700 ...</u> **SEE:** Goldsmith, Valentine Fernande

British Museum. Dept. of Printed Books. <u>Short-title catalogue of Spanish-American books printed before 1601 now in the British Museum.</u> By Henry Thomas. London: Printed by order of the Trustees, 1944.

    CITE AS: BM STC Spanish-Amer., pre-1601

British Museum. Dept. of Printed Books. <u>Short-title catalogues of Portuguese books and of Spanish-American books printed before 1601 now in the British Museum.</u> By H. Thomas. London: B. Quaritch, 1926.

    CITE AS: BM STC Portuguese and Spanish-Amer., pre-1601

British Museum. Dept. of Printed Books. <u>Short-title catalogues of Spanish,
    Spanish-American and Portuguese books printed before 1601 in the British
    Museum.</u> By Henry Thomas. London: British Museum, 1966.

    CITE AS: BM STC Spanish, Spanish-Amer. and Portuguese, pre-1601

British Museum. Dept. of Printed Books. Thomason Collection. <u>Catalogue of
    the pamphlets, books, newspapers, and manuscripts relating to the Civil
    War, the Commonwealth, and Restoration, collected by George Thomason,
    1640-1661.</u> London: Printed by order of the Trustees, 1908.

    CITE AS: Thomason Coll.

British Museum. Dept. of Prints and Drawings. <u>Catalogue of prints and draw-
    ings in the British Museum: Division I, political and personal satires.</u>
    Vols. 1-4 prepared by F.G. Stephens; v. 5-11 by M.D. George. London:
    Printed by order of the Trustees, 1870-1954. Reprint. London: Published
    for the Trustees of the British Museum by British Museum Publications
    Limited, 1978.

    CITE AS: George

British Museum. Dept. of Prints and Drawings. <u>Franks bequest: catalogue of
    British and American book plates bequeathed to the Trustees of the
    British Museum by Sir Augustus Wollaston Franks.</u> London: Printed by
    order of the Trustees, 1903-04.

    CITE AS: Franks bequest

<u>The British union-catalogue of early music printed before the year 1801: a
    record of the holdings of over one hundred libraries throughout the
    British Isles.</u> Editor: Edith B. Schnapper. London: Butterworths Scien-
    tific Publications, 1957.

    CITE AS: BUCEM

Brown, John Carter. <u>Bibliotheca Americana: a catalogue of books relating to
    North and South America in the library of John Carter Brown of Provi-
    dence, R.I.</u> Providence: Printed by H.O. Houghton and Co., Cambridge,
    1865-71.

    CITE AS: Brown, J.C. Cat., 1493-1800

Brown, John Carter. Bibliotheca Americana: a catalogue of books relating to North and South America in the library of the late John Carter Brown of Providence, R.I. Providence: Printed by H.O. Houghton and Co., Cambridge, 1875-82.

CITE AS: Brown, J.C. Cat., 1482-1700

Brown University. John Carter Brown Library. Bibliotheca Americana: catalogue of the John Carter Brown Library in Brown University, Providence, Rhode Island. Providence, 1919-31.

CITE AS: JCB Lib. cat., pre-1675

Brown University. John Carter Brown Library. Bibliotheca Americana: catalogue of the John Carter Brown Library in Brown University, books printed 1675-1700. Providence: Brown University Press, 1973.

CITE AS: JCB Lib. cat., 1675-1700

Brown University. John Carter Brown Library. Bibliotheca Americana: catalogue of the John Carter Brown Library in Brown University, short-title list of additions, books printed 1471-1700. Providence: Brown University Press, 1973.

CITE AS: JCB Lib. cat., additions 1471-1700

Brunet, Jacques Charles. Manual de libraire et de l'amateur de livres. 5. éd., originale entièrement refondue et augm. d'un tiers par l'auteur ... Paris: Firmin Didot frères, fils et cie, 1860-65.
----- ----- Supplément. Par MM. P. Deschamps et G. Brunet. 1878-80.

CITE AS: Brunet

Buck, Solon Justus. Travel and description, 1765-1865, together with a list of county histories, atlases, and biographical collections and a list of territorial and state laws. Springfield, Ill.: The Trustees of the Illinois State Historical Library, 1914. Reprint. New York: B. Franklin, 1971.

CITE AS: Buck, S.J. Travel

Burndy Library, Norwalk, Conn. Heralds of science, as represented by two hundred epochal books and pamphlets selected from the Burndy Library. Norwalk, 1955. Reprint. Cambridge, Mass.: M.I.T. Press, 1969.

CITE AS: Burndy. Science

Caillet, Albert Louis. <u>Manuel bibliographique des sciences psychiques ou occultes.</u> Paris: L. Dorbon, 1912.

    CITE AS: Caillet, A.L. Sciences psychiques

Cambridge. University. Library. <u>A catalogue of the fifteenth-century printed books in the University Library, Cambridge.</u> Comp. by J.C.T. Oates. Cambridge: University Press, 1954.

    CITE AS: Oates

Cambridge. University. Library. <u>Comedias sueltas in Cambridge University Library: a descriptive catalogue.</u> Comp. by A.J.C. Bainton. Cambridge: University Library, 1977.

    CITE AS: Cambridge. Sueltas

Cambridge. University. Library. <u>Early English printed books in the University Library, Cambridge (1475-1640).</u> Comp. by Charles Edward Sayle. Cambridge: University Press, 1900-07. Reprint. New York: Johnson Reprint Corp., 1971.

    CITE AS: Sayle

Cambridge. University. Library. Bradshaw Irish Collection. <u>A catalogue of the Bradshaw Collection of Irish books in the University Library, Cambridge.</u> Cambridge: Printed for the University Library and to be had of B. Quaritch, 1916.

    CITE AS: Bradshaw Irish Coll.

Campbell, Marinus Frederik Andries Gerardus. <u>Annales de la typographie néerlandaise au XV siècle.</u> La Haye: M. Nijhoff, 1874.
    ----- ----- <u>1.-4. supplément.</u> 1878-90.

    CITE AS: Campbell

Canney, Margaret, and Knott, David. <u>Catalogue of the Goldsmiths' Library ...</u>
    SEE: London. University. Goldsmiths' Library of Economic Literature

Carter, Harry Graham, and Vervliet, Hendrik D.L. <u>Civilité types.</u> London: Published for the Oxford Bibliographical Society by the Oxford U.P., 1966.

    CITE AS: Carter & Vervliet

Carter, John, and Muir, Percy H. <u>Printing and the mind of man: a descriptive</u>
<u>catalogue illustrating the impact of print on the evolution of Western</u>
<u>civilization during five centuries.</u> London: Cassell; New York: Holt
Rinehart & Winston, 1967.

CITE AS: PMM

Carteret, Léopold. <u>Le trésor du bibliophile: livres illustrés modernes, 1875</u>
<u>à 1945.</u> Paris: L. Carteret, 1946-48.

CITE AS: Carteret, L. Trésor, 1875-1945

Carteret, Léopold. <u>Le trésor du bibliophile romantique et moderne, 1801-1875.</u>
Par L. Carteret. Éd. rev., corr. et augm. Paris: L. Carteret, 1924-28.
Reprint. Paris: Editions du Vexin français, 1976.

CITE AS: Carteret, L. Trésor, 1801-1875

Case, Arthur Ellicott. <u>A bibliography of English poetical miscellanies,</u>
<u>1521-1750.</u> Oxford: Printed for the Bibliographical Society at the Uni-
versity Press, 1935 (for 1929). Reprint. Folcroft, Pa.: Folcroft Library Editions, 1970.

CITE AS: Case, A.E. Poetical miscellanies

Castan, Auguste. <u>Catalogue des incunables de la bibliothèque publique de</u>
<u>Besançon.</u> **SEE:** Besançon, France. Bibliothèque municipale

Caswell, Jean, and Sipkov, Ivan. <u>The coutumes of France in the Library of</u>
<u>Congress...</u> **SEE:** United States. Library of Congress. European Law
Division

<u>A Checklist of American imprints, 1830-</u>   . Metuchen, N.J.: Scarecrow Press,
1972-

CITE AS: Checklist Amer. imprints

Church, Elihu Dwight. <u>A catalogue of books, consisting of English literature</u>
<u>and miscellanea, including many original editions of Shakespeare, forming</u>
<u>a part of the library of E.D. Church.</u> Comp. and annotated by George
Watson Cole. New York: Dodd, Mead and Co., 1909.

CITE AS: Church, E.D. Engl. lit.

Church, Elihu Dwight. A catalogue of books relating to the discovery and
    early history of North and South America forming a part of the library of
    E.D. Church. Comp. and annotated by George Watson Cole. New York: Dodd,
    Mead and Co.; Cambridge: University Press, 1907.

    CITE AS: Church, E.D. Discovery

Cioranescu, Alexandre. Bibliographie de la littérature française du dix-
    huitième siècle. Paris: Editions du Centre national de la recherche
    scientifique, 1969.

    CITE AS: Cioranescu, A. 18. s.

Cioranescu, Alexandre. Bibliographie de la littérature française du dix-
    septième siècle. Paris: Editions du Centre national de la recherche
    scientifique, 1965-66.

    CITE AS: Cioranescu, A. 17. s.

Cioranescu, Alexandre. Bibliographie de la littérature française du seizième
    siècle. Collaboration et préface de V.-L. Saulnier. Paris: C. Klinck-
    sieck, 1959.

    CITE AS: Cioranescu, A. 16. s.

Clark, Thomas Dionysius. Travels in the Old South: a bibliography. Norman:
    University of Oklahoma Press, 1956-59.

    CITE AS: Clark, T.D. Old South

Cockle, Maurice James Draffen. A bibliography of military books up to 1642
    and of contemporary foreign works. London: Simpkin, Marshall, Hamilton,
    Kent, 1900. Reprint. "2nd ed." London: Holland Press, 1957.

    CITE AS: Cockle, M.J.D. Military books

Cockx-Indestege, Elly. Belgica typographica 1541-1600: catalogue librorum
    impressorum ab anno 1541 ad annum 1600 in regionibus quae nunc Regni
    Belgarum partes sunt. [Auctores] Elly Cockx-Indestege et Geneviève
    Glorieux. Nieuwkoop: B. de Graaf, 1968-

    CITE AS: Cockx-Indestege, E. Belgica typographica

Cohen, Henry. Guide de l'amateur de livres à gravures du XVIIIe siècle. 6.
    éd., rev., cor., et augm. par Seymour de Ricci. Paris: A. Rouquette, 1912.

    CITE AS: Cohen-De Ricci

Colas, René. _Bibliographie générale du costume et de la mode._ Paris: R.
Colas, 1933. Reprint. New York: Hacker Books, 1963 & 1969.

    CITE AS: Colas, R. Costume

Cole, George Watson. _A catalogue of books ... forming a part of the library
of E.D. Church._ **SEE:** Church, Elihu Dwight

Collins, Douglas Cecil. _A handlist of news pamphlets, 1590-1610._ London:
South-West Essex Technical College, 1943.

    CITE AS: Collins, D.C. News pamphlets

Columbia University. Libraries. Avery Architectural Library. _Catalog of the
Avery Memorial Architectural Library of Columbia University._ 2nd ed.,
enl. Boston: G.K. Hall, 1968.

    CITE AS: Avery Lib. (2nd ed.)

Copenhagen. Kongelige Bibliotek. _Katalog over det Kongelige Biblioteks
inkunabler._ Ved Victor Madsen. København: Levin & Munksgaard,
1935-63.

    CITE AS: Madsen

Copinger, Walter Arthur. _Supplement to Hain's Repertorium bibliographicum._
Berlin: J. Altmann, 1926. Reprint. Milano: Görlich, 1950.

    CITE AS: Copinger _or_ Hain-Copinger (as appropriate)

Cox, Edward Godfrey. _A reference guide to the literature of travel, including
voyages, geographical descriptions, adventures, shipwrecks and expedi-
tions._ Seattle: The University of Washington, 1935-49. Reprint. New
York: Greenwood Press, 1969.

    CITE AS: Cox, E.G. Travel

Craig, Mary Elizabeth. _The Scottish periodical press, 1750-1789._ Edinburgh
and London: Oliver and Boyd, 1931.

    CITE AS: Craig, M.E. Scottish periodicals

Crandall, Marjorie Lyle. Confederate imprints: a checklist based principally on the collections of the Boston Athenaeum. Boston: Boston Athenaeum, 1955.

CITE AS: Crandall, M.L. Confederate imprints

Crane, Ronald Salmon, and Kaye, Frederick Benjamin. A census of British news-papers and periodicals, 1620-1800. Chapel Hill, N.C.: The University of North Carolina Press; London: Cambridge University Press, 1927.

CITE AS: Crane & Kaye

Cranfield, Geoffrey Alan. A hand-list of English provincial newspapers and periodicals, 1700-1760. Cambridge: Bowes and Bowes, 1961.

CITE AS: Cranfield, G.A. Engl. provincial newspapers

Crawford, James Ludovic Lindsay, 26th Earl of. A bibliography of royal pro-clamations of the Tudor and Stuart sovereigns and of others published under authority 1485-1714: with an historical essay on their origin and use. Bibliotheca Lindesiana. Oxford: Printed by the Clarendon Press, 1910. Reprint. New York: B. Franklin, 1967.

CITE AS: Crawford, J.L.L. Royal proclamations, 1485-1714

Crawford, James Ludovic Lindsay, 26th Earl of. Bibliotheca Lindesiana ... Catalogue of the printed books preserved at Haigh Hall, Wigan, co. pal. Lancast. Aberdeen: Aberdeen University Press, 1910.

CITE AS: Crawford, J.L.L. Cat. of printed books

Crawford, James Ludovic Lindsay, 26th Earl of. Handlist of proclamations issued by Royal and other constitutional authorities 1714-1910, George I to Edward VII, together with an index of names and places. Bibliotheca Lindesiana. Wigan: Roger and Rennick, 1913.

CITE AS: Crawford, J.L.L. Royal proclamations, 1714-1910

Currey, L.W. Science fiction and fantasy authors: a bibliography of first printings of their fiction and selected nonfiction. Boston: G.K. Hall, 1979.

CITE AS: Currey, L.W. Science fiction

Dahl, Folke. <u>A bibliography of English corantos and periodical newsbooks,</u> <u>1620-1642.</u> London: Bibliographical Society, 1952. Reprint. Boston: Longwood Press, 1977.

CITE AS: Dahl, F. Engl. corantos

Dahl, Folke. <u>Dutch corantos, 1618-1650: a bibliography.</u> The Hague: Konink- lijke Bibliotheek, 1946.

CITE AS: Dahl, F. Dutch corantos

Day, Cyrus Lawrence, and Murrie, Eleanore Boswell. <u>English song-books, 1651-</u> <u>1702: a bibliography with a firstline index of songs.</u> London: Printed for the Bibliographical Society at the University Press, Oxford, 1940. Reprints. Folcroft, Pa.: Folcroft Library Editions, 1975. Norwood, Pa.: Norwood Editions, 1976. Philadelphia: R. West, 1977.

CITE AS: Day & Murray. Songbooks

Dean, Bashford. <u>A bibliography of fishes.</u> New York: American Museum of Natural History, 1916-23. Reprint. New York: Russell & Russell, 1962.

CITE AS: Dean, B. Fishes

Desgraves, Louis. <u>Répertoire bibliographique des livres imprimés en France au</u> <u>XVIIe siècle.</u> Baden-Baden: V. Koerner, 1978-

CITE AS: Desgraves, L. Rép. 17. s.

Dichter, Harry, and Shapiro, Elliott. <u>Early American sheet music, its lure</u> <u>and its lore, 1768-1889; including a directory of early American music</u> <u>publishers.</u> New York: Bowker, 1941. Reprint, with corrections. New York: Dover Publications, 1977.

CITE AS: Dichter & Shapiro

Drake, Milton. <u>Almanacs of the United States.</u> New York: Scarecrow Press, 1962.

CITE AS: Drake, M. Almanacs

Duff, Edward Gordon. <u>Fifteenth century English books: a bibliography of books and documents printed in England and of books for the English market printed abroad.</u> London: Printed for the Bibliographical Society at the Oxford University Press, 1917. Reprints. Folcroft, Pa.: Folcroft Library Editions, 1974. Norwood, Pa.: Norwood Editions, 1977. Philadelphia: R. West, 1978.

    CITE AS: Duff

Durling, Richard J. <u>A catalogue of sixteenth century printed books in the National Library of Medicine.</u> **SEE:** United States. National Library of Medicine

Duveen, Denis I. <u>Bibliotheca alchemica et chemica: an annotated catalogue of printed books on alchemy, chemistry and cognate subjects in the library of Denis I. Duveen.</u> London: E. Weil, 1949.

    CITE AS: Duveen, D.I. Alchemica et chemica

Edelman, Hendrik. <u>Dutch-American bibliography 1693-1794: a descriptive catalog of Dutch-language books, pamphlets and almanacs printed in America.</u> Nieuwkoop: B. de Graaf, 1974.

    CITE AS: Edelman, H. Dutch-Amer. bib.

Esdaile, Arundell James Kennedy. <u>A list of English tales and prose romances printed before 1740.</u> London: Printed for the Bibliographical Society by Blades, East & Blades, 1912. Reprints. New York: B. Franklin, 1971. Norwood, Pa.: Norwood Editions, 1973. Folcroft, Pa.: Folcroft Library Editions, 1974. Philadelphia: R. West, 1977.

    CITE AS: Esdaile, A.J.K. Tales

Estreicher, Karol Jósef Teofil. <u>Bibliografia polska.</u> Kraków: W Druk. Uniw. Jagiellońskiego. 1870-

    CITE AS: Estreicher

Estreicher, Karol Jósef Teofil. <u>Bibliografia polska XIX stulecia: lata 1881-1900.</u> Kraków: Nakł. Spółki Księgarzy Polskich, 1906-16.

    CITE AS: Estreicher, K.J.T. Bib. polska, 1881-1900

Estreicher, Karol Jósef Teofil. <u>Bibliografia polska XIX stulecia.</u> Wyd. 2. Kraków: Pánstwowe Wudawn. Naukowe, Oddział w Krakowie, 1959-

    CITE AS: Estreicher, K.J.T. Bib. polska, 19. stulecia (Wyd. 2)

European Americana: a chronological guide to works printed in Europe relating to the Americas, 1493-1776. Ed. by John Alden with the assistance of Dennis C. Landis. New York: Readex Books, 1980-

CITE AS: Alden, J.E. European Americana

Evans, Charles. American bibliography: a chronological dictionary of all books, pamphlets, and periodical publications printed in the United States of America from the genesis of printing in 1639 down to and including the year 1820. Chicago: Priv. print. for the author by the Blakely Press, 1903-59. Reprints. New York: P. Smith, 1941-59. Metuchen, N.J.: Mini-Print Corp., 1967.

CITE AS: Evans

Ferguson, John Alexander. Bibliography of Australia. Sydney: Angus and Robertson, 1941-69. Reprint. Canberra: National Library of Australia, 1975-

CITE AS: Ferguson, J.A. Australia

Field, Thomas Warren. An essay towards an Indian bibliography: being a catalogue of books relating to the history, antiquities, languages, customs, religion, wars, literature, and origin of the American Indians, in the library of Thomas W. Field. New York: Scribner, Armstrong, and Co., 1873. Reprint. Detroit: Gale Research Co., 1967.

CITE AS: Field, T.W. Indian bib.

Field Museum of Natural History, Chicago. Edward E. Ayer Ornithological Library. Catalogue of the Edward E. Ayer Ornithological Library. By John Todd Zimmer. Chicago: The Museum, 1926. Reprint. New York: Arno Press, 1974.

CITE AS: Zimmer, J.T. Ayer Lib.

First printings of American authors: contributions toward descriptive checklists. Matthew J. Bruccoli, series editor. Detroit: Gale Research Co., 1977-79.

CITE AS: First printings of Amer. authors

Flake, Chad J. A Mormon bibliography, 1830-1930: books, pamphlets, periodicals, and broadsides relating to the first century of Mormonism. Salt Lake City: University of Utah Press, 1978.

CITE AS: Flake, C.J. Mormon bib.

Folger Shakespeare Library. Catalog of printed books of the Folger Shake-
    speare Library, Washington, D.C. Boston: G.K. Hall, 1970.
    -----First supplement. 1976.

    CITE AS: Folger. Printed books

Ford, Worthington Chauncey. Broadsides, ballads, &c. printed in Massachusetts
    1639-1800. Boston: The Massachusetts Historical Society, 1922.

    CITE AS: Ford, W.C. Broadsides

Foxon, David Fairweather. English verse 1701-1750: a catalogue of separately
    printed poems with notes on contemporary collected editions. London and
    New York: Cambridge University Press, 1975.

    CITE AS: Foxon

Frank, Joseph. The beginnings of the English newspaper, 1620-1660. Cam-
    bridge, Mass.: Harvard University Press, 1961.

    CITE AS: Frank, J. Engl. newspaper

Freeman, Rosemary. English emblem books. London: Chatto & Windus, 1948.
    Reprint. New York: Octagon Books, 1966.

    CITE AS: Freeman, R. Engl. emblem books

Fuchs, Georg Friedrich Christian. Repertorium der chemischen Literatur von
    494 vor Christi Geburt bis 1806 in chronol. Ordnung aufgestellt. Hildes-
    heim and New York: Olms, 1974.

    CITE AS: Fuchs, G.F.C. Chemische Lit.

Funck, M. Le livre belge à gravures. Paris and Brussels: C. Van Oest, 1925.

    CITE AS: Funck, M. Livre belge

Gamba, Bartolommeo. Serie dei testi di lingua. 4. ed. Venice: Gondoliere,
    1839.

    CITE AS: Gamba, B. Testi di lingua

García Icazbalceta, Joaquín. Bibliografía mexicana del siglo XVI: catálogo razonado de libros impresos en México de 1539 a 1600. Nueva ed., por Agustín Millares Carlo. México: Fondo de Cultura Económica, 1954.

CITE AS: García Icazbalceta, J. Bib. mexicana (1954 ed.)

Garrison, Fielding Hudson. A medical bibliography (Garrison and Morton): an annotated check-list of texts illustrating the history of medicine. By Leslie T. Morton. 3rd ed. Philadelphia: Lippincott, 1970.

CITE AS: Garrison-Morton (3rd ed.)

Gartrell, Ellen. Electricity, magnetism, and animal magnetism: a checklist of printed sources, 1600-1850. Wilmington, Del.: Scholarly Resources, 1975.

CITE AS: Gartrell, E. Electricity

Gesamtkatalog der Wiegendrucke. Herausgegeben von der Kommission für den Gesamtkatalog der Wiegendrucke. Leipzig: K.W. Hiersemann, 1925- Reprint. Stuttgart: A. Hiersemann; New York: H.P. Krauss, 1968-

CITE AS: GW

Gillett, Charles Ripley. Catalogue of the McAlpin collection .... SEE: New York (City). Union Theological Seminary.

Gillett, Charles Ripley. The McAlpin collection of British history and theology. New York: Union Theological Seminary, 1924.

CITE AS: Gillett, C.R. McAlpin Coll.

Glasgow. Royal College of Science and Technology. Andersonian Library. Bibliotheca chemica: a catalogue of the alchemical, chemical and pharmaceutical books in the collection of the late James Young. By John Ferguson. Glasgow: J. Maclehose and Sons, 1906. Reprint. London: Derek Verschoyle, Academic and Bibliographical Publications, 1954-

CITE AS: Ferguson, J. Bib. chemica

Goff, Frederick R. Incunabula in American libraries: a third census of fifteenth-century books recorded in North American collections. New York: Bibliographical Society of America, 1964. Reprint. Millwood, N.Y.: Kraus Reprint Co., 1973.
----- ----- A supplement. New York: Bibliographical Society of America, 1972.

CITE AS: Goff

Goldsmith, Valentine Fernande. A short title catalogue of French books, 1601-1700, in the Library of the British Museum. Folkestone: Dawsons, 1969-73. Reprint. Folkestone: Dawsons, 1973.

   CITE AS: BM STC French, 1601-1700

Goldsmith, Valentine Fernande. A short title catalogue of Spanish and Portuguese books, 1601-1700, in the Library of the British Museum. Folkestone: Dawsons, 1974.

   CITE AS: BM STC Spanish and Portuguese, 1601-1700

Grässe, Johann Georg Theodor. Trésor de livres rares et précieux. Berlin: J. Altmann, 1922.

   CITE AS: Grässe

Greely, Adolphus Washington. Public documents of the first fourteen congresses, 1789-1817: papers relating to early congressional documents. Washington: Govt. Print. Off., 1900. Reprint. New York: Johnson Reprint Corp., 1973.
   ----- ----- Supplement. Washington: Govt. Print. Off., 1904.

   CITE AS: Greely, A.W. First 14 congresses

Greg, Walter Wilson. A bibliography of the English printed drama to the Restoration. London: Printed for the Bibliographical Society at the University Press, Oxford, 1939-59. Reprint. London: Bibliographical Society, 1970.

   CITE AS: Greg

Greswell, William Parr. A view of the early Parisian Greek press. Oxford: S. Collingwood, 1833.

   CITE AS: Greswell, W.P. Parisian Greek press

Grolier Club, New York. Catalogue of original and early editions of some of the poetical and prose works of English writers from Langland to Wither. New York: Imprinted for the Cooper Square Publishers, 1963.

   CITE AS: Grolier. Langland to Wither

Grolier Club, New York. <u>Catalogue of original and early editions of some of the poetical and prose works of English writers from Wither to Prior.</u> New York: Imprinted for the Cooper Square Publishers, 1963.

    CITE AS: Grolier. Wither to Prior

Grolier Club, New York. <u>One hundred books famous in English literature, with facsimiles of the title pages and an introduction by George E. Woodberry.</u> New York: The Grolier Club, 1902.

    CITE AS: Grolier. 100 Engl. books

Grolier Club, New York. <u>One hundred books famous in science ...</u> **SEE:** Horblit, Harrison D.

Grolier Club, New York. <u>One hundred influential American books printed before 1900: catalogue and addresses: exhibition at the Grolier Club, April eighteenth-June sixteenth, 1946.</u> New York: The Grolier Club, 1947.

    CITE AS: Grolier. 100 Amer. books

Gross, Charles. <u>A bibliography of British municipal history, including gilds and Parliamentary representation.</u> 2nd ed. Leicester: Leicester University Press, 1966.

    CITE AS: Gross, C. Brit. municipal history (2nd ed.)

Guarnaschelli, Teresa Maria, and Valenziani, E. <u>Indice generale degli incunaboli delle biblioteche d'Italia.</u> Roma: La Libreria dello stato, 1943-72.

    CITE AS: IGI

Guerra, Francisco. <u>American medical bibliography, 1639-1783.</u> New York: L.C. Harper, 1962.

    CITE AS: Guerra, F. Amer. medical bib.

Gumuchian et compagnie, booksellers, Paris. <u>Les livres de l'enfance du XV. au XIX. siècle.</u> Préface de Paul Gavault. Paris: En vente à la librairie Gumuchian & cie, [1931?]

    CITE AS: Gumuchian

Haebler, Konrad. Bibliografía ibérica del siglo XV. The Hague and Leipzig:
    M. Nijhoff, etc., 1903-17. Reprint. New York: B. Franklin, 1963.

    CITE AS: Haebler, K. Bib. ibérica

Hagen, Hermann August. Bibliotheca entomologica: die Literatur über das ganze
    Gebiet der Entomologie bis zum Jahre 1862. Leipzig: W. Engelmann, 1862-63.

    CITE AS: Hagen, H.A. Bib. entomologica

Hague. Koninklijke Bibliotheek. Catalogus van de pamfletten-verzameling
    berustende in de Koninklijke Bibliotheek. Bewerkt door Dr. W.P.C.
    Knuttel. 's Gravenhage: Algemeene Landsdrukkerij, 1889-1919.

    CITE AS: Knuttel

Hain, Ludwig Friedrich Theodor. Repertorium bibliographicum, in quo libri
    omnes ab arte typographica inventa usque ad annum MD. typis expressi,
    ordine alphabetico vel simpliciter enumeratur vel adcuratius recensentur.
    Stuttgart: J.G. Cotta, etc., 1826-38. Reprint. Milano: Görlich, 1948.

    CITE AS: Hain

Halkett, Samuel, and Laing, John. Dictionary of anonymous and pseudonymous
    English literature. New and enl. ed., by J. Kennedy, W.A. Smith, and
    A.F. Johnson. Edinburgh: Oliver and Boyd, 1926-62.

    CITE AS: Halkett & Laing (2nd ed.)

Halkett, Samuel, and Laing, John. Dictionary of anonymous and pseudonymous
    publications in the English language. 3rd ed., ed. by John Horden.
    Harlow: Longman, 1980-

    CITE AS: Halkett & Laing (3rd ed.)

Hammelmann, Hanns A. Book illustrators in eighteenth-century England. Ed.
    and completed by T.S.R. Boase. New Haven: Published for the Paul Mellon
    Centre for Studies in British Art (London) by Yale University Press, 1975.

    CITE AS: Hammelmann, H.A. Book illustrators 18th cent. England

Hanson, Laurence William. Comtemporary printed sources for British and Irish
    economic history, 1702-1750. Cambridge: University Press, 1963.

    CITE AS: Hanson

Harrisse, Henry. <u>Bibliotheca Americana vetustissima: a description of works</u> <u>relating to America, published between the years 1492 and 1551.</u> New York: G.P. Philes, 1866.
----- ----- <u>Additions.</u> Paris: Tross; Leipzig: Imprimerie W. Drugulin, 1872.

    CITE AS: Harrisse, H. Americana

Harvard University. Graduate School of Business Administration. Baker Library. Kress Library of Business and Economics. <u>Catalogue: with data</u> <u>upon cognate items in other Harvard libraries.</u> Boston: Baker Library, Harvard Graduate School of Business Administration, 1940-67.

    CITE AS: Kress Lib.

Harvard University. Library. Dept. of Printing and Graphic Arts. <u>Catalogue</u> <u>of books and manuscripts.</u> Pt. 1: <u>French 16th century books.</u> Comp. by Ruth Mortimer under the supervision of Philip Hofer and William A. Jackson. Pt. 2: <u>Italian 16th century books.</u> Comp. by Ruth Mortimer. Cambridge: Belknap Press of Harvard University Press, 1964-

    CITE AS: Mortimer, R. French 16th cent.
             Mortimer, R. Italian 16th cent.

Harvard University. Library. Dept. of Printing and Graphic Arts. <u>Sixteenth-</u> <u>century architectural books from Italy and France: [exhibition] June-</u> <u>September 1971.</u> Cambridge, 1971.

    CITE AS: Harvard. Architectural books

Harwell, Richard Barksdale. <u>More Confederate imprints.</u> Richmond: Virginia State Library, 1957.

    CITE AS: Harwell, R.B. Confederate imprints

Heal, Ambrose. <u>The English writing-masters and their copy-books, 1570-1880: a</u> <u>biographical dictionary & a bibliography, with an introduction on the</u> <u>development of handwriting by Stanley Morison.</u> Cambridge: University Press, 1931.

    CITE AS: Heal, A. Engl. writing-masters

Heartman, Charles Frederick. <u>American primers, Indian primers, Royal primers,</u> <u>and thirty-seven other types of non-New England primers issued prior to</u> <u>1830: a bibliographical checklist.</u> Highland Park, N.J.: Printed for H.B. Weiss, 1935.

    CITE AS: Heartman, C.F. Non-New England primers

Heartman, Charles Frederick. The New England primer issued prior to 1830: a
    bibliographical check-list for the more easy attaining the true knowledge
    of this book. New York: R.R. Bowker Co., 1934.

    CITE AS: Heartman, C.F. New England primer

Hebrew Union College-Jewish Institute of Religion. Library. Jewish Ameri-
    cana: a catalogue of books and articles ... found in the Library of the
    Hebrew Union College-Jewish Institute of Religion in Cincinnati: a sup-
    plement to A.S.W. Rosenbach: An American Jewish bibliography. Cincin-
    nati: American Jewish Archives, 1954.

    CITE AS: Hebrew Union College. Jewish Americana

Henderson, Robert William. Early American sport: a check-list of books by
    American and foreign authors published in America prior to 1860, in-
    cluding sporting songs. 3rd ed., rev. and enl. Rutherford: Farleigh
    Dickenson University Press, 1977.

    CITE AS: Henderson, R.W. Amer. sport (3rd ed.)

Henrey, Blanche. British botanical and horticultural literature before 1800.
    London and New York: Oxford University Press, 1975.

    CITE AS: Henrey, B. Brit. botanical lit.

Herbert, Arthur Sumner. Historical catalogue of printed editions of the Eng-
    lish Bible, 1525-1961. Rev. and expanded from the edition of T.H. Darlow
    and H.F. Moule, 1903. London: British & Foreign Bible Society; New York:
    The American Bible Society, 1968.

    CITE AS: Herbert, A.S. Engl. Bible

Hill, Frank Pierce. American plays printed 1714-1830: a bibliographical re-
    cord. Stanford University, Calif.: Stanford University Press; London: H.
    Milford, Oxford University Press, 1934. Reprints. New York: B. Blom,
    1968. New York: B. Franklin, 1970.

    CITE AS: Hill, F.P. Amer. plays

Hills, Margaret Thorndike. The English Bible in America: a bibliography of
    editions of the Bible & the New Testament published in America, 1777-
    1957. Reprinted with corrections & revisions. New York: American
    Bible Society, 1962.

    CITE AS: Hills, M.T. Engl. Bible in Amer.

Hispanic Society of America. <u>Printed books, 1468-1700, in the Hispanic So-</u>
<u>ciety of America: a listing.</u> By Clara Louisa Penney. New York, 1965.

   CITE AS: Hispanic Society. Printed books, 1468-1700

Hitchcock, Henry Russell. <u>American architectural books: a list of books,</u>
<u>portfolios, and pamphlets on architecture and related subjects published</u>
<u>in America before 1895.</u> New expanded ed., with a new introd. by Adolf K.
Placzek; and included as an appendix: Chronological short-title list of
Henry-Russell Hitch[c]ock's American architectural books, comp. under
the direction of William H. Jordy, and A listing of architectural periodicals before 1895. New York: Da Capo Press, 1976.

   CITE AS: Hitchcock, H.R. Amer. architectural books

Hoe, Robert. <u>Catalogue of the library of Robert Hoe of New York: illuminated</u>
<u>manuscripts, incunabula, historical bindings, early English literature,</u>
<u>rare Americana, French illustrated books, eighteenth century English</u>
<u>authors, autographs, manuscripts, etc. ... To be sold by auction ... by</u>
<u>the Anderson Auction Co., New York.</u> New York: D. Taylor & Co., 1911-
1912.

   CITE AS: Hoe, R. Auction cat.

Horblit, Harrison D. <u>One hundred books famous in science: based on an exhi-</u>
<u>bition held at the Grolier Club.</u> By Harrison D. Horblit. New York,
1964.

   CITE AS: Horblit, H.D. Grolier 100 science books

Hoskins, Janina W. <u>Early and rare Polonica of the 15th-17th centuries in</u>
<u>American libraries: a bibliographical survey.</u> Boston: G.K. Hall, 1973.

   CITE AS: Hoskins, J.W. Polonica

Houzeau, Jean Charles, and Lancaster, A. <u>Bibliographie générale de l'astro-</u>
<u>nomie jusqu'en 1880.</u> Nouv. éd., avec introd. et table des auteurs par
D.W. Dewhirst. London: Holland Press, 1964.

   CITE AS: Houzeau & Lancaster. Astronomie (1964 ed.)

Howes, Wright. <u>U.S.iana, 1650-1950: a selective bibliography in which are</u>
<u>described 11,620 uncommon and significant books relating to the conti-</u>
<u>nental portion of the United States.</u> Rev. and enl. [i.e. 2nd] ed. New
York: Bowker for the Newberry Library, 1962. Reprint. New York: Bowker,
1978.

   CITE AS: Howes, W. U.S.iana (2nd ed.)

Hubach, Robert Rogers. <u>Early Midwestern travel narratives: an annotated bib-liography, 1634-1850.</u> Detroit: Wayne State University Press, 1961.

    CITE AS: Hubach, R.R. Midwestern travel

Hunt, Rachel McMasters Miller. <u>Catalogue of botanical books in the collection of Rachel McMasters Miller Hunt.</u> Comp. by Jane Quinby. Pittsburgh: Hunt Botanical Library. 1958-61.

    CITE AS: Hunt botanical cat.

Huth, Henry. <u>Catalogue of the famous library of printed books, illuminated manucripts, autograph letters and engravings collected by Henry Huth, and since maintained and augmented by his son, Alfred H. Huth ... The printed books and illuminated manuscripts ... sold by auction by Messrs. Sotheby, Wilkinson & Hodge, auctioneers.</u> London: Dryden Press, J. Davy and Sons, 1911-20.

    CITE AS: Huth, H. Auction cat.

<u>Index Aureliensis: catalogus librorum sedecimo saeculo impressorum.</u> Aureliae Aquensis, 1962-

    CITE AS: Index Aureliensis

<u>International inventory of musical sources = Répertoire international des sources musicales.</u> München, etc.: G. Henle, etc., 1960-

    CITE AS: RISM

Isaac, Francis Swinton. <u>An index to the early printed books in the British Museum. Part II. MDI-MDXX. Section II. Italy. Section III. Switzer-land and eastern Europe.</u> London: Bernard Quaritch, 1938.

    CITE AS: Isaac
    (Note: For items in Proctor, use the citation form under that entry.)

Johns Hopkins University. John Work Garrett Library. <u>The Fowler architec-tural collection of Johns Hopkins University: catalogue.</u> Comp. by Law-rence Hall Fowler and Elizabeth Baer. Baltimore: Evergreen House Foun-dation, 1961.

    CITE AS: Fowler

Johnson, Merle de Vore. Merle Johnson's American first editions. 4th ed.,
    rev. and enl. by Jacob Blanck. New York: Bowker, 1942. Reprint. Cam-
    bridge, Mass.: Research Classics, 1962.

    CITE AS: Johnson, M. de V. First editions (4th ed.)

Kansas. University. Libraries. A catalogue of the Ellis collection of orni-
    thological books in the University of Kansas Libraries. Comp. by
    Robert M. Mengel. Lawrence, 1972-

    CITE AS: Ellis Coll.

Kaplan, Louis. A bibliography of American autobiographies. Madison: Uni-
    versity of Wisconsin Press, 1961.

    CITE AS: Kaplan, L. Autobiographies

Karpinski, Louis Charles. Bibliography of mathematical works printed in Amer-
    ica through 1850. Ann Arbor: The University of Michigan Press; London:
    H. Milford, Oxford University Press, 1940.

    CITE AS: Karpinski, L.C. Mathematical works

Klebs, Arnold Carl. Incunabula scientifica et medica: short title list.
    Bruges: The Saint Catherine Press, 1938. Reprint. Hildesheim: G. Olms,
    1963.

    CITE AS: Klebs

Koeman, Cornelis. Atlantes Neerlandici: bibliography of terrestrial, mari-
    time, and celestial atlases and pilot books, published in the Netherlands
    up to 1800. Amsterdam: Theatrum Orbis Terrarum, 1967-71.

    CITE AS: Koeman, C. Atlantes Neerlandici

Kronenberg, Maria Elizabeth. Campbell's Annales de la typographie néer-
    landaise au XV. siècle: contributions to a new edition. The Hague: M.
    Nijhoff, 1956.

    CITE AS: Kronenberg or Campbell-Kronenberg (as appropriate)

Kronenberg, Maria Elizabeth. Nederlandsche bibliographie van 1500 tot 1540.
    SEE: Nijhoff, Wouter

Lancour, Harold. _American art auction catalogues, 1785-1942: a union list._ New York: New York Public Library, 1944.

CITE AS: Lancour, H. Art auction cats.

Landwehr, John. _Dutch emblem books: a bibliography._ Utrecht: Haentjens Dekker & Gumbert, 1962.

CITE AS: Landwehr, J. Dutch emblem books

Landwehr, John. _Emblem books in the Low Countries, 1554-1949: a bibliography._ Utrecht: Haentjens Dekker & Gumbert, 1970.

CITE AS: Landwehr, J. Emblem books in the Low Countries

Landwehr, John. _German emblem books 1531-1888: a bibliography._ Utrecht: Haentjens Dekker & Gumbert; Leiden: Sijthoff, 1972.

CITE AS: Landwehr, J. German emblem books

Lathem, Edward Connery. _Chronological tables of American newspapers, 1690-1820._ Worcester, Mass.: American Antiquarian Society, 1972.

CITE AS: Lathem, E.C. Amer. newspapers

Leclerc, Charles. _Bibliotheca Americana: histoire, géographie, voyages, archéologie et linguistique des deux Amériques et des îles Philippines._ Paris: Maison-Neuve et cie, 1878.
----- ----- _Supplément._ n. 1, Novembre 1881-n. 2, 1881-87.

CITE AS: Leclerc, C. Bib. Americana

Legrand, Émile Louis Jean. _Bibliographie hellénique, ou Description raisonnée des ouvrages publiés en grec par des Grecs au XVe et XVIe siècles._ Paris: E. Leroux, 1885-1906. Reprint. Bruxelles: Culture et civilisation, 1963.

CITE AS: Legrand, E.L.J. Bib. hellénique 15.-16. s.

Legrand, Émile Louis Jean. _Bibliographie hellénique, ou Description raisonnée des ouvrages publiés par des Grecs au dix-septième siècle._ Paris: A. Picard et fils, 1894-96; J. Maisonneuve, 1903. Reprints. New Rochelle, N.Y.: Caratzas, [1977?]. Bruxelles: Culture et civilisation, 1963.

CITE AS: Legrand, E.L.J. Bib. hellénique 17. s.

Legrand, Émile Louis Jean. Bibliographie hellénique, ou Description raisonnée des ouvrages publiés par des Grecs au dix-huitième siècle. Paris: Garnier frères, 1818-28. Reprints. New Rochelle, N.Y.: Caratzas, [1977?] Bruxelles: Culture et civilisation, 1963.

CITE AS: Legrand, E.L.J. Bib. hellénique 18. s.

Lepper, Gary M. A bibliographical introduction to seventy-five modern American authors. Berkeley, Calif.: Serendipity Books, 1976.

CITE AS: Lepper, G.M. Modern Amer. authors

Lindsay, Robert O., and Neu, John. Mazarinades: a checklist of copies in major collections in the United States. Metuchen, N.J.: Scarecrow Press, 1972.

CITE AS: Lindsay & Neu. Mazarinades

London. University. Goldsmiths' Company's Library of Economic Literature. Catalogue of the Goldsmiths' Library of Economic Literature. Comp. by Margaret Canney and David Knott. London: Cambridge University Press, 1970-

CITE AS: Goldsmiths' Lib. cat.

Lowens, Irving. A bibliography of songsters printed in America before 1821. Worcester, Mass.: American Antiquarian Society, 1976.

CITE AS: Lowens, I. Songsters

Lowenstein, Eleanor. Bibliography of American cookery books, 1742-1860. 3rd ed. Worcester, Mass.: American Antiquarian Society, 1972.

CITE AS: Lowenstein, E. Amer. cookery (3rd ed.)

Lowndes, William Thomas. The bibliographer's manual of English literature, containing an account of rare, curious, and useful books, published in or relating to Great Britain and Ireland, from the invention of printing. New ed., rev., cor., and enl., with an appendix relating to the books of literary and scientific societies, by Henry G. Bohn. London: G. Bell & Sons, 1871. Reprint. Detroit: Gale Research Co., 1967.

CITE AS: Lowndes

MacLean, John Patterson. A bibliography of Shaker literature, with an intro-
     ductory study of the writings and publications pertaining to Ohio be-
     lievers. Columbus: F.J. Heer, 1905. Reprint. New York: B. Franklin,
     1971.

     CITE AS: MacLean, J.P. Shaker lit.

Maclean, Virginia. A short-title catalogue of household and cookery books
     published in the English tongue 1701-1800. London: Prospect; Charlottes-
     ville, Va.: distributed by University Press of Virginia, 1981.

     CITE AS: Maclean, V. Household and cookery books

MacPhail, Ian. Alchemy and the occult ... SEE: Yale University. Library.
     Beinecke Rare Book and Manuscript Library.

Madan, Falconer. Oxford books: a bibliography of printed works relating to
     the University and City of Oxford or printed or published there. Oxford:
     Clarendon Press, 1895-1931.

     CITE AS: Madan

Mahé, Raymond. Bibliographie des livres de luxe de 1900 à 1928 inclus.
     Paris: René Kieffer, 1931-43.

     CITE AS: Mahé, R. Livres de luxe

Martin, John. A bibliographical catalogue of privately printed books. 2nd
     ed. London, 1854. Reprint. New York: B. Franklin, 1970.

     CITE AS: Martin, J. Privately printed books (2nd ed.)

McBurney, William Harlin. A check list of English prose fiction, 1700-1739.
     Cambridge: Harvard University Press, 1960.

     CITE AS: McBurney, W.H. Engl. prose fiction

McCoy, Ralph Edward. Freedom of the press: an annotated bibliography. Car-
     bondale: Southern Illinois University Press, 1968.
     ----- ----- Ten-year supplement (1967-1977). 1979.

     CITE AS: McCoy, R.E. Freedom

McDade, Thomas M. The annals of murder: a bibliography of books and pamphlets on American murders from colonial times to 1900. 1st ed. Norman: University of Oklahoma Press, 1961.

CITE AS: McDade, T.M. Murder

McGill University, Montreal. Library. The Lawrence Lande collection of Canadiana in the Redpath Library of McGill University: a bibliography. Collected, arranged, and annotated by Lawrence Lande. Montreal: Lawrence Lande Foundation for Canadian Historical Research, 1965. ----- Rare and unusual Canadiana: first supplement to the Lande bibliography. Comp. by Lawrence Lande. Montreal: McGill University, 1971.

CITE AS: Lande Coll.

McKay, George Leslie. American book auction catalogues, 1713-1934: a union list. New York: The New York Public Library, 1937.

CITE AS: McKay, G.L. Amer. auction cats.

McLeod, William Reynolds, and McLeod, V.B. Anglo-Scottish tracts, 1701-1714: a descriptive checklist. Lawrence: University of Kansas Libraries, 1979.

CITE AS: McLeod & McLeod. Anglo-Scottish tracts

Mebane, John. Books relating to the Civil War: a priced check list, including regimental histories, Lincolniana, and Confederate imprints. New York: T. Yoseloff, 1963.

CITE AS: Mebane, J. Civil War

Medina, José Toribio. Biblioteca hispano-americana (1493-1810). Santiago de Chile, 1898-1907. Reprint. Amsterdam: N. Israel, 1968.

CITE AS: Medina, J.T. Bib. hispano-americana

Medina, José Toribio. Biblioteca hispano-chilena (1523-1817). Santiago de Chile: The author, 1897-99. Reprint. Amsterdam: N. Israel, 1965.

CITE AS: Medina, J.T. Bib. hispano-chilena

Medina, José Toribio. La imprenta en la Puebla de los Angeles (1640-1821). Santiago de Chile: Imprenta Cervantes, 1908. Reprint. Amsterdam: N. Israel, 1964.

CITE AS: Medina, J.T. Puebla de los Angeles

Medina, José Toribio. <u>La imprenta en México (1539-1821).</u> Santiago de Chile: The author, 1907-12. Reprint. Amsterdam: N. Israel, 1965.

    CITE AS: Medina, J.T. México

Mellon, Paul. <u>Alchemy and the occult ...</u> **SEE:** Yale University. Library. Beinecke Rare Book and Manuscript Library.

Melvin, Frank E. <u>A bibliography of the Frank E. Melvin collection ...</u> **SEE:** Saricks, Ambrose.

Mendelssohn, Sidney. <u>A South African bibliography to the year 1925 = N Suid-Afrikaanse bibliografie tot die Jaar 1925: being a revision and continuation of Sidney Mendelssohn's South African bibliography (1910).</u> Ed. at the South African Library, Cape Town. London: Mansell, 1979.

    CITE AS: Mendelssohn, S. South African bib.

Mengel, Robert M. <u>A catalogue of the Ellis collection ...</u> **SEE:** Kansas. University. Libraries

Metzdorf, Robert F. <u>The Tinker library ...</u> **SEE:** Tinker, Chaucey Brewster

Michel, Suzanne P., and Michel, Paul-Henri. <u>Répertoire des ouvrages imprimés en langue italienne au XVIIe siècle.</u> Firenze: L.S. Olschki, 1970-

    CITE AS: Michel & Michel

Moraes, Rubens Borba de. <u>Bibliografia brasileira do período colonial.</u> São Paulo: Instituto de Estudos Brasileiros, 1969.

    CITE AS: Moraes, R.B. de. Bib. brasileira do período colonial

Moraes, Rubens Borba de. <u>Bibliographia Brasiliana: a bibliographical essay.</u> Amsterdam: Colibris Editora, 1958.

    CITE AS: Moraes, R.B. de. Bib. Brasiliana

Moreau, Brigitte. <u>Inventaire chronologique des éditions parisiennes du XVIe siècle ... d'après les manuscrits de Philippe Renouard.</u> Paris: Imprimerie municipale, 1972-

    CITE AS: Moreau

Moreau, Célestin. Bibliographie des mazarinades. Paris: J. Renouard,
    1850-51. Reprint. New York: B. Franklin, 1965.
    ----- [Supplements]. By Moreau, Van der Haeghen, Socard, and Labadie.
    1859-1904.

    CITE AS: Moreau, C. Mazarinades

Morgan, William Thomas. A bibliography of British history (1700-1715) with
    special reference to the reign of Queen Anne. Bloomington, Ind., 1934-
    42. Reprint. New York: B. Franklin, 1972-73.

    CITE AS: Morgan

Mottelay, Paul Fleury. Bibliographical history of electricity & magnetism,
    chronologically arranged. London: C. Griffin, 1922. Reprint. New York:
    Arno Press, 1975.

    CITE AS: Mottelay, P.F. Electricity

Muller, Frederick. Mémoire bibliographique ... SEE: Tiele, Pieter Anton

Muller (Frederick) en Compagnie, Amsterdam. Catalogue of books, maps, plates
    on America and of a remarkable collection of early voyages. Amsterdam:
    F. Muller, 1872-75. Reprint. Amsterdam: N. Israel, 1966.

    CITE AS: Muller, F. Amer.

Munby, Alan Noel Latimer, and Coral, Lenore. British book sale catalogues,
    1676-1800: a union list. London: Mansell, 1977.

    CITE AS: Munby & Coral

Murray, Charles Fairfax. Catalogue of a collection of early French books in
    the library of C. Fairfax Murray. Comp. by Hugh Wm. Davies. London:
    Priv. print., 1910.

    CITE AS: Murray, C.F. French books

Murray, Charles Fairfax. Catalogue of a collection of early German books in
    the library of C. Fairfax Murray. Comp. by Hugh Wm. Davies. London:
    Priv. print., 1913.

    CITE AS: Murray, C.F. German books

National Book League, London. <u>English poetry: an illustrated catalogue of</u>
   <u>first and early editions, exhibited in 1947 at 7 Albemarle Street, Lon-</u>
   <u>don.</u> Comp. and rev. by John Hayward. London: Cambridge Univ. Press,
   1950. Reprint. Westport, Conn.: Greenwood Press, 1975.

   CITE AS: Hayward

<u>National union catalog: a cumulative author list representing Library of Con-</u>
   <u>gress printed cards and titles reported by other American libraries.</u>
   Washington: Library of Congress, 1956-

   CITE AS: NUC 1958-1962
            NUC 1963-1967
            NUC 1968-1972
            NUC 1973-1979
            NUC 1980 [etc.]

<u>National union catalog, pre-1956 imprints: a cumulative author list represent-</u>
   <u>ing Library of Congress printed cards and titles reported by other Ameri-</u>
   <u>can libraries.</u> London: Mansell, 1968-1980.
   ----- <u>Supplement.</u> 1980-1981.

   CITE AS: NUC pre-1956

<u>New Cambridge bibliography of English literature.</u> Ed. by George Watson.
   Cambridge: University Press, 1969-77.

   CITE AS: NCBEL

New York (City). Public Library. Arents Tobacco Collection. <u>Tobacco: a</u>
   <u>catalogue of the books, manuscripts, and engravings acquired since 1942</u>
   <u>in the Arents Tobacco Collection at the New York Public Library, from</u>
   <u>1507 to the present.</u> New York: The New York Public Library, 1958-69.

   CITE AS: Arents Coll.

New York (City). Union Theological Seminary. Library. <u>Catalogue of the</u>
   <u>McAlpin collection of British history and theology.</u> Comp. and ed. by
   Charles Ripley Gillett. New York: Union Theological Seminary, 1927-30.

   CITE AS: McAlpin Coll.

Newberry Library, Chicago. <u>A catalogue of the Everett D. Graff collection of</u>
   <u>Western Americana.</u> Comp. by Colton Storm. Chicago: Published for the
   Newberry Library by the University of Chicago Press, 1968.

   CITE AS: Graff Coll.

Newberry Library, Chicago. A check list of courtesy books in the Newberry library. Comp. by Virgil B. Heltzel. Chicago: The Newberry Library, 1942.

CITE AS: Heltzel, V.B.   Courtesy books in the Newberry

Newberry Library, Chicago. Edward E. Ayer Collection. Narratives of cap-
tivity among the Indians of North America: a list of books and manu-
scripts. Chicago: The Newberry Library, 1912. Reprints. Ann Arbor:
Gryphon Books, 1971. Detroit: Gale Research Co., 1974.
----- ----- Supplement I. By Clara A. Smith. Chicago: The Newberry
Library, 1928.

CITE AS: Ayer Coll.

Newberry Library, Chicago. John M. Wing Foundation. Dictionary catalogue of
the history of printing from the John M. Wing Foundation in the Newberry
Library. Boston: G.K. Hall, 1961.
----- First supplement. 1970.

CITE AS: Wing Foundation

Nielsen, Lauritz Martin. Dansk bibliografi, 1482-1600 med saerligt hensyn til
dansk bogtrykkerkunsts historie. København: Gyldendal, 1919-33.

CITE AS: Nielsen, L.M. Dansk bib.

Nijhoff, Wouter, and Kronenberg, Maria Elizabeth. Nederlandsche bibliographie
van 1500 tot 1540. 's-Gravenhage: M. Nijhoff, 1923-1971.

CITE AS: Nijhoff & Kronenberg

Nissen, Claus. Die botanische Buchillustration: ihre Geschichte und Bibliographie. 2. Aufl., durchgesehener und verb. Abdruck der zweibändigen
Erstaufl., ergänzt durch ein Supplement. Stuttgart: Hiersemann, 1966.

CITE AS: Nissen, C. Botanische Buchillustration (2. Aufl.)

Nissen, Claus. Die illustrierten Vogelbücher: ihre Geschichte und Bibliographie. Stuttgart: Hiersemann Verlag, 1953. Reprint. Stuttgart:
Hiersemann Verlag, 1976.

CITE AS: Nissen, C. Illustrierte Vogelbücher

Nissen, Claus. Schöne Fischbücher: kurze Geschichte der ichthyologischen
Illustration: Bibliographie fischkundlicher Abbildungswerke. Stuttgart:
L. Hempe Verlag, 1951.

CITE AS: Nissen, C. Schöne Fischbücher

Nissen, Claus. Schöne Vogelbücher: ein Überblick der ornithologischen Illustration, nebst Bibliographie. Wien, etc.: H. Reichner, 1936.

  CITE AS: Nissen, C. Schöne Vogelbücher

Nissen, Claus. Die zoologische Buchillustration: ihre Bibliographie und Geschichte. Stuttgart: Hiersemann, 1966-

  CITE AS: Nissen, C. Zoologische Buchillustration

Norton, Frederick John. A descriptive catalogue of printing in Spain and Portugal, 1501-1520. Cambridge and New York: Cambridge University Press, 1978.

  CITE AS: Norton, F.J. Spain and Portugal

Norton, Frederick John. Italian printers, 1501-1520: an annotated list with an introduction. London: Bowes and Bowes, 1958.

  CITE AS: Norton, F.J. Italian printers

Olivier, Eugène; Hermal, Georges; and Roton, R. de. Manuel de l'amateur de reliures armoriées françaises. Paris: C. Bosse, 1924-35.

  CITE AS: Olivier, E. Reliures armoriées

Osler, William. Bibliotheca Osleriana: a catalogue of books illustrating the history of medicine and science, collected, arranged and annotated by Sir William Osler and bequeathed to McGill University. Oxford: Clarendon Press, 1929. Reprint. Montreal: McGill-Queen's University Press, 1969.

  CITE AS: Osler, W. Bib. Osleriana

Oxford. University. Bodleian Library. A catalogue of English newspapers and periodicals in the Bodleian Library, 1622-1800. By R.T. Milford and D.M. Sutherland. London: Printed for the Oxford Bibliographical Society at the Oxford University Press, 1936.

  CITE AS: Bodleian newspapers

Palau y Dulcet, Antonio. <u>Manual del librero hispano-americano: inventario
bibliográfico de la producción científica y literaria de España y de la
América latina desde la invención de la imprenta hasta nuestros dias, con
el valor comercial de todos los artículos descritos.</u> Barcelona: Libreria
anticuaria, 1923-27.

CITE AS: Palau y Dulcet

Palau y Dulcet, Antonio. <u>Manual del librero hispano-americano: bibliografía
general española e hispano-americana desde la invención de la imprenta
hasta nuestros tiempos, con el valor comercial de los impresos descritos.</u>
2. ed. corr. y aumentada por el autor. Barcelona: A. Palau, 1948-77.

CITE AS: Palau y Dulcet (2nd ed.)

Palmer, Philip Motley. <u>German works on America, 1492-1800.</u> Berkeley: University of California Press, 1952.

CITE AS: Palmer, P.M. German works on Amer.

Panzer, Georg Wolfgang Franz. <u>Annales typographici ab artis inventae origine
ad annum MD.</u> Nuremburg: J.B. Zeh, 1793-1803.

CITE AS: Panzer

Paris. Bibliothèque nationale. Département des imprimés. <u>Catalogue général
des livres imprimés de la Bibliothèque nationale: auteurs.</u> Paris: Impr.
nationale, 1897-
----- Paris. Bibliothèque nationale. <u>Catalogue général des livres imprimés: auteurs, collectivités-auteurs, anonymes, 1960-1969.</u> 1972-

CITE AS: BN
          BN (1960-69)

Paris. Bibliothèque nationale. Département des imprimés. <u>Catalogue général
des livres imprimés de la Bibliothèque nationale: actes royaux.</u> Paris:
Impr. nationale, 1910-60.

CITE AS: BN Actes royaux

Paris. Université. Bibliothèque. <u>Catalogue de la réserve XVIe siècle (1501-
1540) de la bibliothèque de l'Université de Paris.</u> Par Charles Beaulieux. Paris: H. Champion, 1910. Reprint. New York: B. Franklin, 1969.
----- ----- Supplément et suite (1541-1550). 1923.

CITE AS: Paris. Université. Cat., 1501-1540

Parke-Bernet Galleries, inc., New York. The celebrated collection of Americana formed by the late Thomas Winthrop Streeter. New York, 1966-69.

   CITE AS: Streeter Americana

Parsons, Wilfrid. Early Catholic Americana: a list of books and other works by Catholic authors in the United States, 1729-1830. New York: Macmillan, 1939. Reprints. Boston: Milford House, 1973. Boston: Longwood Press, 1977.
----- List of additions and corrections to Early Catholic Americana.
Contribution of French translations (1724-1820) by Forrest Bowe. New York: Franco-Americana, 1952.

   CITE AS: Parsons, W. Catholic Americana

Pellechet, Marie Léontine Catherine. Catalogue général des incunables des bibliothèques publiques de France. Paris: A. Picard, 1897-1909. Reprint. Nendeln, Liechtenstein: Kraus-Thomson Organization Ltd., 1970.

   CITE AS: Pellechet

Pennsylvania. University. Libraries. Sixteenth-century imprints in the libraries of the University of Pennsylvania. By M.A. Shaaber. Philadelphia: University of Pennsylvania Press, 1976.

   CITE AS: Shaaber, M.A. 16th cent. imprints

Penny, Clara Louisa. Printed books, 1468-1700, in the Hispanic Society of America ... SEE: Hispanic Society of America

Perrins, Charles William Dyson. Italian book-illustrations and early printing: a catalogue of early Italian books in the library of C.W. Dyson Perrins. Oxford: University Press, etc., 1914.

   CITE AS: Perrins, C.W.D. Italian books

Pforzheimer, Carl Howard. The Carl H. Pforzheimer library: English literature, 1475-1700. New York: Priv. print., The Morrill Press, 1940.

   CITE AS: Pforzheimer

Philadelphia. Library Company. Afro-Americana, 1553-1906: author catalog of the Library Company of Philadelphia and the Historical Society of Pennsylvania. Boston: G.K. Hall, 1973.

   CITE AS: Lib. Company. Afro-Americana

Pia, Pascal. <u>Les Livres de l'Enfer: bibliographie critique des ouvrages érotiques dans leurs différentes éditions du XVIe siècle à nos jours.</u>
Paris: C. Coulet et A. Faure, 1978.

CITE AS: Pia, P. Livres de l'Enfer

Polain, Louis. <u>Catalogue des livres imprimés au quinzième siècle des bibliothèques de Belgique.</u> Bruxelles: Pour la Société des bibliophiles & icon-
ophiles de Belgique, 1932.

CITE AS: Polain

Pollard, Alfred William, and Redgrave, G.R. <u>A short-title catalogue of books
printed in England, Scotland & Ireland and of English books printed
abroad, 1475-1640.</u> London: Bibliographical Society, 1926. Reprint.
London: Bibliographical Society, 1969.

CITE AS: STC

Pollard, Alfred William, and Redgrave, G.R. <u>A short-title catalogue of books
printed in England, Scotland & Ireland and of English books printed
abroad, 1475-1640.</u> 2nd ed., rev. & enl., begun by W.A. Jackson & F.S.
Ferguson, completed by Katharine F. Pantzer. London: Bibliographical
Society, 1976-

CITE AS: STC (2nd ed.)

Praet, Joseph Basile Bernard van. <u>Catalogue des livres imprimés sur vélin de
la bibliothèque de roi.</u> Paris: De Bure frères, 1822-28. Reprint. New
York: B. Franklin, 1965.

CITE AS: Praet, J.B.B. van. Vélin, bib. du roi

Praet, Joseph Basile Bernard van. <u>Catalogue des livres imprimés sur vélin,
qui se trouvent dans des bibliothèques tant publiques que particulières.</u>
Paris: De Bure frères, 1824-28. Reprint. New York: B. Franklin, 1965.

CITE AS: Praet, J.B.B. van. Vélin, bib. publiques

Princeton University. Library. <u>Early American book illustrators and wood
engravers, 1670-1870: a catalogue of a collection of American books,
illustrated for the most part with woodcuts and wood engravings, in the
Princeton Library.</u> With an introductory sketch by Sinclair Hamilton.
Princeton, N.J.: Princeton University Press, 1968.

CITE AS: Hamilton, S. Amer. book illustrators (1968 ed.)

Pritzel, Georg August. <u>Thesaurus literaturae botanicae omnium gentium.</u>
    Leipzig: F.Z. Brockhaus, 1872-77. Reprint. Milano: Görlich, 1950.

    CITE AS: Pritzel

Proctor, Robert George Collier. <u>An index to the early printed books in the</u>
    <u>British Museum.</u> London: Kegan Paul, Trench, Trübner, 1898-1903.

    CITE AS: Proctor
    (Note: For items in Isaac, use the citation form under that entry.)

Quérard, Joseph-Marie. <u>La France littéraire.</u> Paris: Didot père et fils,
    1827-64. Reprint. Paris: Maisonneuve and Larose, 1964.

    CITE AS: Quérard

Quinby, Jane. <u>Catalogue of botanical books in the collection of Rachel</u>
    <u>McMasters Miller Hunt ...</u> **SEE:** Hunt, Rachel McMasters Miller

Rader, Jesse Lee. <u>South of forty, from the Mississippi to the Rio Grande: a</u>
    <u>bibliography.</u> 1st ed. Norman: University of Oklahoma Press, 1947.

    CITE AS: Rader, J.L. South of forty

Ransom, Will. <u>Private presses and their books.</u> New York: R.R. Bowker Co.,
    1929. Reprint. New York: AMS Press, 1976.

    CITE AS: Ransom, W. Private presses

Ray, Gordon Norton. <u>The illustrator and the book in England from 1790 to</u>
    <u>1914.</u> New York: Pierpont Morgan Library, 1976.

    CITE AS: Ray, G.N. Illustrator and the book in England

Reginald, R. <u>Science fiction and fantasy literature: a checklist, 1700-1974:</u>
    <u>with Contemporary science fiction authors II.</u> Detroit: Gale Research
    Co., 1979.

    CITE AS: Reginald, R. Science fiction

Reichling, Dietrich. Appendices ad Hainii-Copingeri Repertorium bibliogra-
    phicum. Munich: I. Rosenthal, 1905-11. Reprint. Milano: Görlich Edi-
    tore, 1953.
    ----- ----- Supplementum. Monasterii Gvestphalorum: Theissingianis,
    1914.

    CITE AS: Reichling, Hain-Reichling, Hain-Copinger-Reichling, or Copinger-
        Reichling (as appropriate)

Renouard, Philippe. Inventaire chronologique des éditions parisiennes du XVIe
    siècle ... SEE: Moreau, Brigitte.

Répertoire bibliographique des livres imprimés en France au seizième siècle.
    Baden-Baden: Librairie Heitz: Editions Valentin Koerner, 1968-

    CITE AS: Rép. 16. s.

Répertoire international des sources musicales. SEE: International inventory
    of musical sources ...

Riccardi, Pietro. Biblioteca matematica italiana dalla origine della stampa
    ai primi anni del secolo XIX. Modena: Società tipografica, 1873-93.
    ----- Correzioni ed aggiunte, serie VII. Modena: Società tipografica
    modense, 1928. Reprint. Milano: Görlich, 1952.

    CITE AS: Riccardi, P. Bib. matematica

Rink, Evald. Technical Americana: a checklist of technical publications
    printed before 1831. Millwood, N.Y.: Kraus International Publications,
    1981.

    CITE AS: Rink, E. Technical Americana

Ripley, S. Dillon. Ornithological books in the Yale University Library ...
    SEE: Yale University. Library

Ritter, François. SEE ALSO: Strasbourg. Bibliothèque de la ville, etc.

Ritter, François. Catalogue des incunables ne figurant pas à la Bibliothèque
    nationale et universitaire de Strasbourg. Répertoire bibliographique des
    livres imprimés en Alsace aux XVe et XVIe siècles, 3. ptie. Strasbourg:
    P.H. Heitz, 1960.

    CITE AS: Ritter, F. Incun. ne figurant pas à la Bib. nat. de Strasbourg

Ritter, François. Catalogue des livres du XVIe siècle ne figurant pas à la
    Bibliothèque nationale et universitaire de Strasbourg. Répertoire bib-
    liographique des livres imprimés en Alsace aux XVe et XVIe siècles, 4.
    ptie. Strasbourg: P.H. Heitz, 1960.

    CITE AS: Ritter, F. Livres du 16. s. ne figurant pas à la Bib. nat.
        de Strasbourg

Rochedieu, Charles Alfred Emmanuel. Bibliography of French translations of
    English works, 1700-1800. Chicago: University of Chicago Press, 1948.

    CITE AS: Rochedieu, C.A.E. French translations

Romaine, Lawrence B. A guide to American trade catalogs, 1744-1900. New
    York: R.R. Bowker, 1960. Reprint. New York: Arno Press, 1976.

    CITE AS: Romaine, L.B. Amer. trade cats.

Ronalds, Francis. Catalogue of books and papers relating to electricity,
    magnetism, the electric telegraph, &c., including the Ronalds Library.
    London and New York: E. & F.N. Spon, 1880.

    CITE AS: Ronalds, F. Electricity

Rosenbach, Abraham Simon Wolf. An American Jewish bibliography: being a list
    of books and pamphlets by Jews, or relating to them, printed in the
    United States from the establishment of the press in the colonies until
    1850. Baltimore: American Jewish Historical Society, 1926.

    CITE AS: Rosenbach, A.S.W. Amer. Jewish bib.
    (Note: The supplement by the Hebrew Union College-Jewish Institute of
    Religion is entered separately under that heading.)

Rosenbach, Abraham Simon Wolf. Early American children's books, with biblio-
    graphical descriptions of the books in his private collection. Portland,
    Me.: The Southworth Press, 1933. Reprints. New York: Kraus Reprint
    Corp., 1966. New York: Dover Publications, 1971.

    CITE AS: Rosenbach, A.S.W. Children's books

Rothschild, Nathan James Edouard. Catalogue des livres composant la biblio-
    thèque de feu M. la baron James de Rothschild. Paris: D. Morgand, 1884-
    1920.

    CITE AS: Rothschild, N.J.E. Cat.

Rothschild, Nathaniel Mayer Victor. The Rothschild library: a catalogue of
    the collection of eighteenth-century printed books and manuscripts formed
    by Lord Rothschild. Cambridge [Eng.]: Priv. print. at the University
    Press, 1954.

    CITE AS: Rothschild

Rowlands, William. Cambrian bibliography: containing an account of the books
    printed in the Welsh language, or relating to Wales, from the year 1546
    to the end of the eighteenth century, with biographical notices. Ed. and
    enl. by the Rev. D. Silvan Evans. Llanidloes: Print. and pub. by J.
    Pryse, 1869. Reprint. Amsterdam: Meridian Pub. Co., 1970.

    CITE AS: Rowlands, W. Cambrian bib.

Sabin, Joseph. A dictionary of books relating to America, from its discovery
    to the present time. New York, 1868-1936. Reprints. New York: Mini-
    Print Corp., 196-? Metuchen, N.J.: Scarecrow Press, 1966.

    CITE AS: Sabin

Sadleir, Michael. XIX century fiction: a bibliographical record based on his
    own collection. London: Constable; Berkeley: University of California
    Press, 1951. Reprint. New York: Cooper Square Publishers, 1969.

    CITE AS: Sadleir, M. 19th cent. fiction

Sander, Max. Le livre à figures italien depuis 1467 jusqu'à 1530: essai de sa
    bibliographie et de son histoire. New York: G.E. Stechert, 1941 [i.e.
    1941-43]
    ----- Supplément. By Carlo Enrico Rava. Milan: U. Hoepli, 1969.

    CITE AS: Sander

Saricks, Ambrose. A bibliography of the Frank E. Melvin collection of pam-
    phlets of the French Revolution in the University of Kansas Libraries.
    Lawrence: University of Kansas Libraries, 1960.

    CITE AS: Saricks, A. Melvin Coll.

Schreiber, Wilhelm Ludwig. Handbuch der Holz- und Metallschnitte des XV.
    Jahrhunderts = Manuel de l'amateur de la gravure sur bois et sur metal au
    XVe siècle. 3. Aufl. Vollständiger Neudruck des Gesamtwerkes. Stutt-
    gart: A. Hiersemann; Nendeln: Kraus Reprint, 1969.

    CITE AS: Schreiber, W.L. Handbuch (3. Aufl.)

Schwerdt, Charles Francis George Richard. <u>Hunting, hawking, shooting, illustrated in a catalogue of books, manuscripts, prints, and drawings, collected by C.F.G.R. Schwerdt.</u> London: Priv. print. for the author by
Waterlow & Sons ltd., 1928-37.

    CITE AS: Schwerdt, C.F.G.R. Hunting

Seidensticker, Oswald. <u>The first century of German printing in America,
1728-1830.</u> Philadelphia: Schaefer & Koradi, 1893. Reprints. New York:
Kraus Reprint Corp., 1966. Millwood, N.Y.: Kraus Reprint, 1980.
----- <u>A new supplement.</u> By Gerhard Friedrich. Philadelphia, 1940.

    CITE AS: Seidensticker, O. German printing

Shaaber, Matthias Adam. <u>Check-list of works of British authors printed
abroad, in languages other than English, to 1641.</u> New York: Bibliographical Society of America, 1975.

    CITE AS: Shaaber, M.A. Brit. authors

Shaw, Ralph Robert, and Shoemaker, Richard H. <u>American bibliography: a pre-
liminary checklist for 1801-1819.</u> New York: Scarecrow Press, 1958-66.

    CITE AS: Shaw & Shoemaker

Shipton, Clifford Kenyon, and Mooney, James E. <u>National index of American
imprints throught 1800: the short-title Evans.</u> Worcester, Mass.: American Antiquarian Society, 1969.

    CITE AS: Shipton & Mooney

Shoemaker, Richard H. <u>A checklist of American imprints for 1820-1829.</u> New
York: Scarecrow Press, 1964-71.

    CITE AS: Shoemaker

<u>Short-title catalog of books printed in Italy and of books in Italian printed
abroad, 1501-1600, held in selected North American libraries.</u> Robert G.
Marshall, ed. Boston: G.K. Hall, 1970.

    CITE AS: Marshall, R.G. STC Italian

Silva, Innocencio Francisco da. <u>Diccionário bibliográphico portuguez.</u> Lisboa: Na Imprensa nacional, 1858-1923.

    CITE AS: Silva, I.F. da. Diccionário bib. portuguez

Simon, André Louis. <u>Bibliotheca gastronomica: a catalogue of books and docu-
ments on gastronomy: the production, taxation, distribution and consump-
tion of food and drink, their use and abuse in all times and among all
peoples.</u> London: Wine and Food Society, 1953.

CITE AS: Simon, A.L. Bib. gastronomica

Smith, Charles Wesley. <u>Pacific Northwest Americana: a check list of books
and pamphlets relating to the history of the Pacific Northwest.</u> 3rd ed.,
rev. and extended by Isabel Mayhew. Portland, Or.: Binfords & Mort,
1950.

CITE AS: Smith, C.W. Pacific Northwest (3rd ed.)

Smith, David Eugene. <u>Rara arithmetica: a catalogue of the arithmetics written
before the year MDCI with a description of those in the library of George
Arthur Plimpton of New York.</u> 4th ed. New York: Chelsea Publ. Co., 1970.

CITE AS: Smith, D.E. Rara arithmetica (4th ed.)

Smith, Joseph, bookseller. <u>Bibliotheca anti-Quakeriana, or, A catalogue of
books adverse to the Society of Friends, alphabetically arranged, with
biographical notices of the authors.</u> London: J. Smith, 1873. Reprint.
New York: Kraus Reprint Co., 1968.

CITE AS: Smith, J. Anti-Quakeriana

Smith, Joseph, bookseller. <u>A descriptive catalogue of Friends' books, or
books written by members of the Society of Friends, commonly called
Quakers, from their first rise to the present time, interspersed with
critical remarks and ... biographical notices.</u> London: J. Smith, 1867.
----- <u>Supplement.</u> London: E. Hicks, 1893.

CITE AS: Smith, J. Friends' books

Sommervogel, Carlos. <u>Bibliothèque de la Compagnie de Jesus ...</u> **SEE:** Backer,
Augustine de

Sonneck, Oscar George Theodore. <u>A bibliography of early secular American
music (18th century).</u> Rev. and enl. by William Treat Upton. Washington:
The Library of Congress, Music Division, 1945. Reprint. New York: Da
Capo Press, 1964.

CITE AS: Sonneck-Upton

Sonneck, Oscar George Theodore. <u>Catalogue of opera librettos printed before
1800.</u> **SEE:** United States. Library of Congress. Music Division

Spear, Dorothea N. Bibliography of American directories through 1860. Worcester, Mass.: American Antiquarian Society, 1961. Reprint. Westport, Conn.: Greenwood Press, 1978.

CITE AS: Spear, D.N. Amer. directories

Spielmann, Percy Edwin. Catalogue of the library of miniature books collected by Percy Edwin Spielmann. London: E. Arnold, 1961.

CITE AS: Spielmann, P.E. Miniature books

Starnes, De Witt Talmage. Renaissance dictionaries, English-Latin and Latin-English. Austin: University of Texas Press, 1954.

CITE AS: Starnes, D.T. Renaissance dictionaries

Starr, Edward Caryl. A Baptist bibliography, being a register of printed material by and about Baptists: including works written against the Baptists. Philadelphia, etc.: Published by the Judson Press for the Samuel Colgate Baptist Historical Collection, Colgate University, etc., 1947-76.

CITE AS: Starr, E.C. Baptist bib.

Stewart, Powell. British newspapers and periodicals, 1632-1800: a descriptive catalogue of a collection at the University of Texas. Austin: University of Texas, 1950.

CITE AS: Stewart, P. Brit. newspapers

Stillwell, Margaret Bingham. The awakening interest in science during the first century of printing, 1450-1550: an annotated checklist of first editions viewed from the angle of their subject content. New York: Bibliographical Society of America, 1970.

CITE AS: Stillwell, M.B. Science

Stillwell, Margaret Bingham. The beginning of the world of books, 1450-1470: a chronological survey of the texts chosen for printing during the first twenty years of the printing arts, with a synopsis of the Gutenberg documents. New York: Bibliographical Society of America, 1972.

CITE AS: Stillwell, M.B. World of books, 1450-1470

Stoddard, Roger Eliot. A catalogue of books and pamphlets unrecorded in Oscar Wegelin's Early American poetry, 1650-1820. Providence, R.I.: Friends of the Library of Brown University, 1969.

   CITE AS: Stoddard, R.E. Unrecorded Wegelin

Strasbourg. Bibliothèque de la ville. Catalogue des incunables et livres du XVIe siècle de la Bibliothèque municipale de Strasbourg. Par François Ritter. Strasbourg: P.H. Heitz, 1948.

   CITE AS: Ritter, F. Incun. de la Bib. municipale de Strasbourg

Strasbourg. Bibliothèque nationale et universitaire. Catalogue des incunables alsaciens de la Bibliothèque nationale et universitaire de Strasbourg. Répertoire bibliographique des livres imprimés en Alsace au 16me siècle, fascicules hors sér. I-V. Par François Ritter. Strasbourg: Heitz, 1938.

   CITE AS: Ritter, F. Incun. alsaciens de la Bib. nat. de Strasbourg

Strasbourg. Bibliothèque nationale et universitaire. Répertoire bibliographique des livres du XVIe siècle qui se trouvent a la Bibliothèque nationale et universitaire de Strasbourg. Par F. Ritter. Strasbourg: P.H. Heitz, 1937-55. Reprint. Naarden: A.W. v. Bekhoven, [1968?]

   CITE AS: Ritter, F. Livres du 16. s. à la Bib. nat. de Strasbourg

Stratman, Carl Joseph. Bibliography of English printed tragedy, 1565-1900. Carbondale: Southern Illinois University Press, 1966.

   CITE AS: Stratman, C.J. Engl. printed tragedy

Summers, Montague. A Gothic bibliography. London: The Fortune Press, 1941. Reprint. London: Fortune Press, 1969.

   CITE AS: Summers, M. Gothic bib.

Sveriges bibliografi 1481-1600. Uppsala: Svenska litteratursällskapet, 1927-33.

   CITE AS: Sveriges bib.

Talvart, Hector, and Place, Joseph. Bibliographie des auteurs modernes de langue française. Paris: Éditions de la Chronique des lettres françaises, 1928-76.

   CITE AS: Talvart & Place. Auteurs modernes

Tchemerzine, Avenir. Bibliographie d'éditions originales et rares d'auteurs français des XVe, XVIe, XVIIe, et XVIIIe siècles. Paris: Plée, 1927-34. Reprints. Teaneck [N.J.]: Somerset House, 1973. Paris: Hermann, 1977.

CITE AS: Tchemerzine

Thomas, Henry. Short-title catalogues of Spanish, Spanish-American, and Portuguese books ... SEE: British Museum. Dept. of Printed Books

Thompson, Lawrence Sidney. The new Sabin: books described by Joseph Sabin and his successors, now described again on the basis of examination of originals, and fully indexed by title, subject, joint authors, and institutions and agencies. Troy, N.Y.: Whitston Pub. Co., 1974-

CITE AS: New Sabin

Thompson, Ralph. American literary annuals & gift books, 1825-1865. New York: H.W. Wilson Co., 1936. Reprint. Hamden, Conn.: Archon Books, 1967.

CITE AS: Thompson, R. Annuals

Thomson, Thomas Richard. Check list of publications on American railroads before 1841: a union list of printed books and pamphlets, including state and federal documents, dealing with charters, by-laws, legislative acts, speeches, debates, land grants, officers' and engineers' reports, travel guides, maps, etc. New York: The New York Public Library, 1942.

CITE AS: Thomson, T.R. Railroads

Tiele, Pieter Anton. Mémoire bibliographique sur les journaux navigateurs néerlandais réimprimés dans les collections de De Bry et de Hulsius et dans les collections hollandaises du XVIIe siècle, et sur les anciennes éditions hollandaises des journaux de navigateurs étrangers, la plupart en la possession de Frédérik Muller à Amsterdam. Amsterdam: F. Muller, 1867. Reprint. Amsterdam: N. Israel, 1960.

CITE AS: Tiele, P.A. Journaux navigateurs

The Times, London. Tercentenary handlist of English & Welsh newspapers, magazines & reviews. London: The Times, 1920.

CITE AS: Times handlist

Tinker, Chauncey Brewster. The Tinker library: a bibliographical catalogue of the books and manuscripts collected by Chauncey Brewster Tinker. Comp. by Robert F. Metzdorf. New Haven: Yale University Library, 1959.

   CITE AS: Tinker lib.

Tissandier, Gaston. Bibliographie aéronautique: catalogue de livres d'histoire, de science, de voyages et de fantaisie, traitant de la navigation aérienne ou des aérostats. Paris: H. Launette et cie, 1887.

   CITE AS: Tissandier, G. Bib. aéronautique

Tomkinson, Geoffrey Stewart. A select bibliography of the principal modern presses, public and private, in Great Britain and Ireland. London: First Edition Club, 1928. Reprint. San Francisco: A. Wofsy Fine Arts, 1975.

   CITE AS: Tomkinson, G.S. Modern presses

Toole-Stott, Raymond. A bibliography of English conjuring. Derby: Harper and Sons, 1976-78.

   CITE AS: Toole-Stott, R. Conjuring

Tooley, Ronald Vere. English books with coloured plates, 1790-1860: a bibliographical account of the most important books illustrated by English artists in colour aquatint and colour lithography. Rev. ed. Folkestone, Eng.: Dawson, 1979.

   CITE AS: Tooley, R.V. Coloured plates (1979 ed.)

Toronto. Public Libraries. Boys and Girls Services. The Osborne collection of early children's books: a catalogue prepared at Boys and Girls House. By Judith St. John. Toronto: Toronto Public Library, 1958-75.

   CITE AS: Osborne Coll.

Tremaine, Marie. A bibliography of Canadian imprints, 1751-1800. Toronto: University of Toronto Press, 1952.

   CITE AS: Tremaine

United States. Library of Congress. European Law Division. The coutumes of France in the Library of Congress: an annotated bibliography. By Jean Caswell and Ivan Sipkov. Washington: Library of Congress, 1977.

   CITE AS: LC coutumes

United States. Library of Congress. Catalogue of early books on music (before 1800). By Julia Gregory and Hazel Bartlett. Prepared under the direction of O.G. Sonneck. Washington: Govt. Print. Off., 1913. Reprint. New York: Da Capo Press, 1969.
----- ----- Supplement. (Books acquired by the Library 1913-1942.) By Hazel Bartlett. With a list of books on music in Chinese and Japanese. Washington, 1944.

CITE AS: Gregory

United States. Library of Congress. A catalog of the gifts of Lessing J. Rosenwald to the Library of Congress, 1943 to 1975. Washington: Library of Congress, 1977.

CITE AS: Rosenwald

United States. Library of Congress. Map Division. A list of geographical atlases in the Library of Congress, with bibliographical notes. Vols. 1-4 comp. under the direction of P.L. Phillips. Washington: Govt. Print. Off., 1909- . Reprint (vols. 1-4). Amsterdam: Theatrum Orbis Terrarum, 1971.

CITE AS: Phillips

United States. Library of Congress. Music Division. Catalogue of opera librettos printed before 1800. Prepared by Oscar George Theodore Sonneck. Washington: Govt. Print. Off., 1914. Reprint. New York: B. Franklin, 1967.

CITE AS: Sonneck, O.G.T. Librettos

United States. Library of Congress. Periodicals Division. A check list of American eighteenth century newspapers in the Library of Congress. Originally comp. by John Van Ness Ingram. New ed., rev. and. enl. under the direction of Henry S. Parsons. Washington: Govt. Print. Off., 1936. Reprint. New York: Greenwood Press, 1968.

CITE AS: LC 18th cent. newspapers (1936 ed.)

United States. Library of Congress. Rare Book Division. Catalog of broadsides in the Rare Book Division. Boston: G.K. Hall, 1972.

CITE AS: LC broadsides

United States. Library of Congress. Rare Book Division. Children's books in the Rare Book Division of the Library of Congress. Totowa, N.J.: Rowman and Littlefield, 1975.

CITE AS: LC children's books

United States. National Library of Medicine. A catalogue of sixteenth century printed books in the National Library of Medicine. Comp. by Richard
J. Durling. Bethesda, Md., 1967.

    CITE AS: NLM 16th cent.

United States. National Library of Medicine. Early American medical imprints: a guide to works printed in the United States, 1668-1820. By
Robert B. Austin. Washington: U.S. Dept. of Health, Education, and Welfare, Public Health Service, 1961.

    CITE AS: Austin, R.B. Early Amer. medical imprints

Vicaire, Georges. Bibliographie gastronomique. Paris: P. Rouquette et fils,
1890.

    CITE AS: Vicaire, G. Bib. gastronomique

Vicaire, Georges. Manuel de l'amateur de livres du XIXe siècle, 1801-1893.
Paris: A. Rouquette, 1894-1920. Reprints. Teaneck [N.J.]: Somerset
House, 1973. New York: B. Franklin, 1973.

    CITE AS: Vicaire, G. Livres du 19. s.

Vindel, Francisco. El arte tipográfico en España durante el siglo XV. Mad-
rid: Ministerio de Asuntos Exteriores, Relaciones Culturales, 1945-51.
----- El arte tipográfico en Cataluña durante el siglo XV: apéndice.
Madrid: Dirección General de Relaciones Culturales, 1954.

    CITE AS: Vindel, F. Arte tipográfico

Vindel, Francisco. Manual gráfico-descriptivo del bibliófilo hispano-americano (1475-1850). Madrid, etc., 1930-31.
----- ----- Suplemento. 1934-

    CITE AS: Vindel, F. Manual

Wagner, Henry Raup. Nueva bibliografía mexicana del siglo XVI, suplemento a
las bibliografías de don Joaquín García Icazbalceta, don José Toribio
Medina y don Nicolás Léon. México: Editorial Polis, 1940 [i.e. 1946]

    CITE AS: Wagner, H.R. Bib. mexicana

Wagner, Henry Raup. The Plains and the Rockies: a bibliography of original narratives of travel and adventure, 1800-1865. Rev. by Charles I. Camp. 3rd ed. Columbus, Ohio: Long's College Book Co., 1953.

    CITE AS: Wagner-Camp

Wagner, Henry Raup. The Spanish Southwest, 1542-1794: an annotated bibliography. Albuquerque: The Quivira Society, 1937. Reprint. New York: Arno Press, 1967.

    CITE AS: Wagner, H.R. Spanish Southwest

Ward, William Smith. Index and finding list of serials published in the British Isles, 1789-1832. Lexington: University of Kentucky Press, 1953.

    CITE AS: Ward, W.S. Index of serials

Weaver, William D. Catalogue of the Wheeler gift ... **SEE:** American Institute of Electrical Engineers. Library.

Wegelin, Oscar. Early American poetry: a compilation of the titles and volumes of verse and broadsides by writers born or residing in North America, north of the Mexican border. New York: P. Smith, 1930.

    CITE AS: Wegelin, O. Amer. poetry

Welch, D'Alte Aldridge. A bibliography of American children's books printed prior to 1821. Worcester, Mass.: American Antiquarian Society, 1972.

    CITE AS: Welch, D.A. Amer. children's books

Wellcome Historical Medical Library, London. A catalogue of printed books in the Wellcome Historical Medical Library. London: Wellcome Historical Medical Library, 1962-

    CITE AS: Wellcome cat. of printed books

Weller, Emil Ottokar. Die falschen und fingierten Druckorte: Repertorium der seit Erfindung der Buchdruckerkunst unter falscher Firma erschienenen deutschen, lateinischen und französischen Schriften. Hildesheim: G. Olms, 1960.
----- Nachträge. 1961.

    CITE AS: Weller, E.O. Falsche Druckorte

White, Gleeson. English illustration, 'The sixties': 1855-70. Westminster: A. Constable, 1897. Reprint. Bath: Kingsmead Reprints, 1970.

   CITE AS: White, G. Engl. illustration

Wiener, Joel H. A descriptive finding list of unstamped British periodicals, 1830-1836. London: Bibliographical Society, 1970.

   CITE AS: Wiener, J.H. Unstamped Brit. periodicals

Wierzbowski, Teodor. Bibliographia Polonica XV ac XVI ss. Varsoviae: C. Kowalewsky, 1889-94.

   CITE AS: Wierzbowski, T. Bib. Polonica

Wiles, Roy McKeen. Freshest advices: early provincial newspapers in England. Columbus: Ohio State University Press, 1965.

   CITE AS: Wiles, R.M. Freshest advices

Williams, Iolo Aneurin. Seven XVIIIth century bibliographies. London: Dulau, 1924. Reprint. New York: B. Franklin, 1968.

   CITE AS: Williams, I.A. 18th cent. bib.

Winans, Robert B. A descriptive checklist of book catalogues separately printed in America, 1693-1800. Worcester: American Antiquarian Society, 1981.

   CITE AS: Winans, R.B. Book cats.

Wing, Donald Goddard. Short-title catalogue of books printed in England, Scotland, Ireland, Wales, and British America, and of English books printed in other countries, 1641-1700. New York: Index Society, 1945-51.

   CITE AS: Wing

Wing, Donald Goddard. Short-title catalogue of books printed in England, Scotland, Ireland, Wales, and British America, and of English books printed in other countries, 1641-1700. 2nd ed., rev. and enl. New York: Index Committee of the Modern Language Association of America, 1972-

   CITE AS: Wing (2nd ed.)

Wisconsin. University. Library. <u>Chemical, medical, and pharmaceutical books printed before 1800, in the collections of the University of Wisconsin Libraries.</u> Ed. by John Neu. Comp. by Samuel Ives, Reese Jenkins, and John Neu. Madison: University of Wisconsin Press, 1965.

CITE AS: Wisconsin. Chemical books

Wise, Thomas James. <u>The Ashley library, a catalogue of printed books, manuscripts, and autograph letters, collected by Thomas James Wise.</u> London: Printed for private circulation only, 1922-36. Reprint. Folkestone: Dawsons of Pall Mall, 1971.

CITE AS: Wise, T.J. Ashley lib.

Wolfe, Richard J. <u>Secular music in America, 1801-1825: a bibliography.</u> New York: The New York Public Library, 1964.

CITE AS: Wolfe, R.J. Secular music.

Wolff, Robert Lee. <u>Nineteenth-century fiction: a bibliographical catalogue based on the collection formed by Robert Lee Wolff.</u> New York: Garland Pub., 1981-

CITE AS: Wolff, R.L. 19th cent. fiction

Wood, Casey Albert. <u>An introduction to the literature of vertebrate zoology: based chiefly on the titles in the Blacker Library of Zoology, the Emma Shearer Wood Library of ornithology, the Bibliotheca Osleriana and other libraries of the McGill University, Montreal.</u> London: Oxford University Press, 1931. Reprint. New York: Arno Press, 1974.

CITE AS: Wood, C. Vertebrate zoology

Wright, Lyle Henry. <u>American fiction, 1774-1850: a contribution toward a bibliography.</u> 2nd rev. ed. San Marino, Calif.: Huntington Library, 1969.

CITE AS: Wright, L.H. Amer. fiction, 1774-1850 (2nd ed.)

Wright, Lyle Henry. <u>American fiction, 1851-1875: a contribution toward a bibliography.</u> San Marino, Calif.: Huntington Library, 1965.

CITE AS: Wright, L.H. Amer. fiction, 1851-1875

Wright, Lyle Henry. American fiction, 1876-1900: a contribution toward a bibliography. San Marino, Calif.: Huntington Library, 1966.

    CITE AS: Wright, L.H. Amer. fiction, 1876-1900

Yale University. Library. Ornithological books in the Yale University Library, including the library of William Robertson Coe. Comp. by S. Dillon Ripley and Lynette L. Scribner. New Haven: Yale University Press, 1961.

    CITE AS: Yale. Ornithological books

Yale University. Library. Beinecke Rare Book and Manuscript Library. Alchemy and the occult: a catalogue of books and manuscripts from the collection of Paul and Mary Mellon given to Yale University Library. New Haven: Yale University Library, 1968-77.

    CITE AS: Yale. Alchemy

Yale University. Library. Yale Collection of German Literature. German Baroque literature: a catalogue of the collection in the Yale University Library. By Curt von Faber du Faur. New Haven: Yale University Press, 1958-69.

    CITE AS: Faber du Faur

INDEX TO

STANDARD CITATION FORMS

AAS dictionary cat.

American Antiquarian Society, Worcester, Mass. Library. <u>A dictionary catalog</u> <u>of American books pertaining to the 17th through 19th centuries.</u> West-port, Conn.: Greenwood Pub. Corp., 1971.

Abbey, J.R. Life

Abbey, John Roland. <u>Life in England in aquatint and lithography, 1770-1860:</u> <u>architecture, drawing books, art collections, magazines, navy and army,</u> <u>panoramas, etc., from the library of J.R. Abbey: a bibliographical cat-</u> <u>alogue.</u> London: Priv. print. at the Curwen Press, 1953. Reprint. Folkestone: Dawsons of Pall Mall, 1972.

Abbey, J.R. Scenery

Abbey, John Roland. <u>Scenery of Great Britain and Ireland in aquatint and</u> <u>lithography, 1770-1860, from the library of J.R. Abbey: a bibliographical</u> <u>catalogue.</u> London: Priv. print. at the Curwen Press, 1952. Reprint. Folkestone: Dawsons of Pall Mall, 1972.

Abbey, J.R. Travel

Abbey, John Roland. <u>Travel in aquatint and lithography, 1770-1860, from the</u> <u>library of J.R. Abbey: a bibliographical catalogue.</u> London: Priv. print. at the Curwen Press, 1956-57. Reprint. Folkestone: Dawsons of Pall Mall, 1972.

Adams

Adams, Herbert Mayow. <u>Catalogue of books printed on the continent of Europe,</u> <u>1501-1600, in Cambridge libraries.</u> London: Cambridge University Press, 1967.

Adams, R.F. Six-guns (1969 ed.)

Adams, Ramon Frederick. <u>Six-guns and saddle leather: a bibliography of books</u> <u>and pamphlets on western outlaws and gunmen.</u> New ed., rev. and greatly enl. Norman: University of Oklahoma Press, 1969.

Adams, T.R. Amer. pamphlets

Adams, Thomas Randolph. <u>American independence, the growth of an idea: a bib-</u> <u>liographical study of the American political pamphlets printed between</u> <u>1764 and 1776 dealing with the dispute between Great Britain and her</u> <u>colonies.</u> Providence: Brown University Press, 1965.

Adams, T.R. Brit. pamphlets

Adams, Thomas Randolph. The American controversy: a bibliographical study of the British pamphlets about the American disputes, 1764-1783. Providence: Brown University Press; New York: Bibliographical Society, 1980.

Adomeit, R.E. Thumb Bibles

Adomeit, Ruth E. Three centuries of thumb Bibles: a checklist. New York: Garland, 1980.

Alden, J.E. European Americana

European Americana: a chronological guide to works printed in Europe relating to the Americas, 1493-1776. Ed. by John Alden with the assistance of Dennis C. Landis. New York: Readex Books, 1980-

Aldis, H.G. Scotland

Aldis, Harry Gidney. A list of books printed in Scotland before 1700. Edinburgh: Edinburgh Bibliographical Society, 1904. Reprints. Edinburgh: National Library of Scotland, 1970. New York: B. Franklin, 1970.

Allison & Rogers. Catholic books

Allison, Antony Francis, and Rogers, David Morrison. A catalogue of Catholic books in English printed abroad or secretly in England, 1558-1640. Bognor Regis: Arundel Press, 1956. Reprint. London: W. Dawson, 1964.

Alston, R.C. Engl. language

Alston, R.C. A bibliography of the English language from the invention of printing to the year 1800: a systematic record of writings on English, and on other languages in English, based on the collections of the principal libraries of the world. Leeds, Eng.: Printed for the author by E.J. Arnold, 1965-72.

Anker, J. Bird books

Anker, Jean. Bird books and bird art. Copenhagen: Levin & Munksgaard, 1938. Reprint. New York: Arno Press, 1974.

Arents Coll.

New York (City). Public Library. Arents Tobacco Collection. Tobacco: a catalogue of the books, manuscripts, and engravings acquired since 1942 in the Arents Tobacco Collection at the New York Public Library, from 1507 to the present. New York: The New York Public Library, 1958-69.

Arents, G. Tobacco

Arents, George. Tobacco, its history illustrated by the books, manuscripts, and engravings in the library of George Arents, Jr., together with an introductory essay, a glossary, and bibliographic notes by Jerome E. Brooks. New York: Rosenbach Co., 1937-52.

Arnott, J.F. Engl. theatrical lit.

Arnott, James Fullarton, and Robinson, John William. English theatrical literature, 1559-1900: a bibliography, incorporating Robert W. Lowe's "A bibliographical account of English theatrical literature" published in 1888. London: Society for Theatre Research, 1970.

Artist and the book

Boston. Museum of Fine Arts. The artist & the book, 1860-1960, in Western Europe and the United States. Boston: Museum of Fine Arts; Cambridge, Mass.: Harvard College Library, Dept. of Printing and Graphic Arts, 1961.

Austin, R.B. Early Amer. medical imprints

United States. National Library of Medicine. Early American medical imprints: a guide to works printed in the United States, 1668-1820. By Robert B. Austin. Washington: U.S. Dept. of Health, Education, and Welfare, Public Health Service, 1961.

Avery Lib. (2nd ed.)

Columbia University. Libraries. Avery Architectural Library. Catalog of the Avery Memorial Architectural Library of Columbia University. 2nd ed., enl. Boston: G.K. Hall, 1968.

Ayer Coll.

Newberry Library, Chicago. Edward E. Ayer Collection. Narratives of captivity among the Indians of North America: a list of books and manuscripts. Chicago: The Newberry Library, 1912. Reprints. Ann Arbor: Gryphon Books, 1971. Detroit: Gale Research Co., 1974.
----- ----- Supplement I. By Clara A. Smith. Chicago: The Newberry Library, 1928.

BAL

Blanck, Jacob Nathaniel. <u>Bibliography of American literature.</u> Comp. for the Bibliographical Society of America. New Haven: Yale University Press, 1955-

Backer-Sommervogel

Backer, Augustine de. <u>Bibliothèque de la Compagnie de Jesus.</u> Nouv. éd. par Carlos Sommervogel. Bruxelles: O. Schepens; Paris: A. Picard, 1890-1932. ----- ----- <u>Corrections et additions.</u> Par Ernest-M. Rivière. Toulouse: Rivière, 1911-17.

Barbier, A.A. Ouvrages anonymes

Barbier, Antoine Alexandre. <u>Dictionnaire des ouvrages anonymes.</u> 3. éd., rev. et augm. Paris: P. Daffis, 1872-79. Reprint. Paris: G.P. Maisonneuve & Larose, 1964.

Baudrier, H.L. Bib. lyonnaise

Baudrier, Henri Louis. <u>Bibliographie lyonnaise: recherches sur les imprimeurs, libraires, relieurs et fondeurs de lettres de Lyon au XVIe siècle.</u> Publiées et continuées par J. Baudrier. Lyon: Librairie ancienne d'Auguste Brun, 1895-1921.
----- <u>Table.</u> Par George Tricou. Genève: E. Droz, 1950-52.

Beale, J.H. Engl. law

Beale, Joseph Henry. <u>A bibliography of early English law books.</u> Cambridge: Harvard University Press, 1926.
----- ----- <u>A supplement.</u> 1943.

Berlin. Ornamentstichsammlung

Berlin. Staatliche Kunstbibliothek. <u>Katalog der Ornamentstichsammlung der Staatlichen Kunstbibliothek, Berlin.</u> Berlin: Verlag für Kunstwissenschaft, 1939.

Bersano Begey, M. Cinquecentine piemontesi

Bersano Begey, Marina. <u>Le cinquecentine piemontesi.</u> Torino: Tipografia torinese editrice, 1961-66.

Besançon. Incun.

Besançon, France. Bibliothèque municipale. <u>Catalogue des incunables de la bibliothèque publique de Besançon.</u> Par Auguste Castan. Besançon: J. Dodivers, 1893.

Besterman, T. Art books

Besterman, Theodore. <u>Old art books.</u> London: Maggs Bros. Ltd., 1975.

Bib. Belgica

<u>Bibliotheca Belgica: bibliographie générale des Pays-Bas.</u> Fondée par Ferd. van der Haeghen et publiée sous sa direction. Gand: Vanderpoorten; La Haye: M. Nijhoff, 1880-1923.

Bigmore & Wyman

Bigmore, Edward Clements, and Wyman, C.W.H., comps. <u>A bibliography of printing, with notes and illustrations.</u> London: B. Quaritch, 1880-86. Reprints. New York: P.C. Duschnes, 1945. London: Holland Press; Newark, Del.: Oak Knoll Books, 1978.

Bishop, W.W. Checklist (2nd ed.)

Bishop, William Warner. <u>A checklist of American copies of "Short-title catalogue" books.</u> 2nd ed. Ann Arbor: University of Michigan Press, 1950. Reprint. New York: Greenwood Press, 1968.

Bitting, K.G. Gastronomic bib.

Bitting, Katherine Golden. <u>Gastronomic bibliography.</u> San Francisco, 1939. Reprint. Ann Arbor, Mich.: Gryphon Books, 1971.

BLC

British Library. <u>The British Library general catalogue of printed books to 1975.</u> London: C. Bingley; London and New York: K.G. Saur, 1979-

Block, A. Engl. novel

Block, Andrew. <u>The English novel, 1740-1850: a catalogue including prose romances, short stories, and translations of foreign fiction.</u> London: Grafton & Co., 1939. Reprints. London: Dawsons of Pall Mall; Dobbs Ferry, N.Y.: Oceana, 1967. Westport, Conn.: Greenwood, 1981.

BM
BM (1956-65)
BM (1966-70)

British Museum. Dept. of Printed Books. <u>General catalogue of printed books</u>
<u>to 1955.</u> Photolithographic ed. London: Trustees of the British Museum,
1959-66.
----- ----- <u>Ten-year supplement, 1956-1965.</u> 1968.
----- ----- <u>Five-year supplement, 1966-1970.</u> 1971-72.

BM (compact ed.)

British Museum. Dept. of Printed Books. <u>General catalogue of printed books</u>
<u>to 1955.</u> Compact ed. New York: Readex Microprint Corp., 1967-

BM 15th cent.

British Museum. Dept. of Printed Books. <u>Catalogue of books printed in the</u>
<u>XVth century now in the British Museum.</u> London: Printed by order of the
Trustees, 1908-71.

BM STC Dutch and Flemish, 1470-1600

British Museum. Dept. of Printed Books. <u>Short-title catalogue of books</u>
<u>printed in the Netherlands and Belgium and of Dutch and Flemish books</u>
<u>printed in other countries from 1470 to 1600 now in the British Museum.</u>
London: Trustees of the British Museum, 1965.

BM STC French, 1470-1600

British Museum. Dept. of Printed Books. <u>Short-title catalogue of books</u>
<u>printed in France and of French books printed in other countries from</u>
<u>1470-1600 now in the British Museum.</u> London: Printed by order of the
Trustees, 1924. Reprint. London: British Museum, 1966.

BM STC French, 1601-1700

Goldsmith, Valentine Fernande. <u>A short title catalogue of French books, 1601-</u>
<u>1700, in the Library of the British Museum.</u> Folkestone: Dawsons, 1969-
73. Reprint. Folkestone: Dawsons, 1973.

BM STC German, 1455-1600

British Museum. Dept. of Printed Books. <u>Short-title catalogue of books</u>
<u>printed in the German-speaking countries and German books printed in</u>
<u>other countries from 1455 to 1600 now in the British Museum.</u> London:
Trustees of the British Museum, 1962.

BM STC Italian, 1465-1600

    British Museum. Dept. of Printed Books. <u>Short-title catalogue of books
        printed in Italy and of Italian books printed in other countries from
        1465 to 1600 now in the British Museum.</u> London: Trustees of the British
        Museum, 1958

BM STC Portuguese and Spanish-Amer., pre-1601

    British Museum. Dept. of Printed Books. <u>Short-title catalogues of Portuguese
        books and of Spanish-American books printed before 1601 now in the Bri-
        tish Museum.</u> By H. Thomas. London: B. Quaritch, 1926.

BM STC Spanish and Portuguese, 1601-1700

    Goldsmith, Valentine Fernande. <u>A short title catalogue of Spanish and Por-
        tuguese books, 1601-1700, in the Library of the British Museum.</u> Folke-
        stone: Dawsons, 1974.

BM STC Spanish, pre-1601

    British Museum. Dept. of Printed Books. <u>Short-title catalogue of books
        printed in Spain and of Spanish books printed elsewhere in Europe before
        1601 now in the British Museum.</u> London: Printed by order of the
        Trustees, 1921.

BM STC Spanish, Spanish-Amer. and Portuguese, pre-1601

    British Museum. Dept. of Printed Books. <u>Short-title catalogues of Spanish,
        Spanish-American and Portuguese books printed before 1601 in the British
        Museum.</u> By Henry Thomas. London: British Museum, 1966.

BM STC Spanish-Amer., pre-1601

    British Museum. Dept. of Printed Books. <u>Short-title catalogue of Spanish-
        American books printed before 1601 now in the British Museum.</u> By Henry
        Thomas. London: Printed by order of the Trustees, 1944.

BN
BN (1960-69)

    Paris. Bibliothèque nationale. Département des imprimés. <u>Catalogue général
        des livres imprimés de la Bibliothèque nationale: auteurs.</u> Paris: Impr.
        nationale, 1897-
        ----- Paris. Bibliothèque nationale. <u>Catalogue général des livres im-
        primés: auteurs, collectivités-auteurs, anonymes, 1960-1969.</u> 1972-

BN Actes royaux

Paris. Bibliothèque nationale. Département des imprimés. <u>Catalogue général</u>
<u>des livres imprimés de la Bibliothèque nationale: actes royaux.</u> Paris:
Impr. nationale, 1910-60.

Bodleian newspapers

Oxford. University. Bodleian Library. <u>A catalogue of English newspapers and</u>
<u>periodicals in the Bodleian Library, 1622-1800.</u> By R.T. Milford and D.M.
Sutherland. London: Printed for the Oxford Bibliographical Society at
the Oxford University Press, 1936.

Bohatta, H. Livres d'Heures (2. Aufl.)

Bohatta, Hanns. <u>Bibliographie der Livres d'Heures (Horae B.M.V.): Officia,</u>
<u>Hortuli Animae, Coronae B.M.V., Rosaria und Cursus B.M.V. des XV. und</u>
<u>XVI. Jahrhunderts.</u> 2. verm. Aufl. Wien: Gilhofer & Ranschburg, 1924.

Bond & Bond

Bond, Richmond Pugh, and Bond, Marjorie N. <u>The Tatler and the Spectator and</u>
<u>the development of the early periodic press in England: a checklist of</u>
<u>the collection of Richmond P. Bond and Marjorie N. Bond.</u> Chapel Hill,
N.C., 1965.

Borchling & Claussen

Borchling, Conrad, and Claussen, Bruno. <u>Niederdeutsche Bibliographie:</u>
<u>Gesamtverzeichnis der niederdeutschen Drucke bis zum Jahre 1800.</u> Neu-
munster: K. Wachholtz Verlag, 1931-36.

Bosanquet, E.F. Almanacks

Bosanquet, Eustace Fulcrand. <u>English printed almanacks and prognostications:</u>
<u>a bibliographical history to the year 1600.</u> London: Printed for the
Bibliographical Society at the Chiswick Press, 1917.
----- ----- <u>Corrigenda and addenda.</u> 1928.

Boyer, M. Texas coll. of sueltas

Boyer, Mildred. <u>The Texas collection of comedias sueltas: a descriptive bib-</u>
<u>liography.</u> Boston: G.K. Hall, 1978.

Bradshaw Irish Coll.

Cambridge. University. Library. Bradshaw Irish Collection. A catalogue of the Bradshaw Collection of Irish books in the University Library, Cambridge. Cambridge: Printed for the University Library and to be had of B. Quaritch, 1916.

Brigham, C.S. Amer. newspapers

Brigham, Clarence Saunders. History and bibliography of American newspapers, 1690-1820. Worcester, Mass.: American Antiquarian Society, 1947. Reprint. Westport, Conn.: Greenwood Press, 1976.
----- ----- Additions and corrections. 1961.

Brinley, G. Cat.

Brinley, George. Catalogue of the American library of the late Mr. George Brinley, of Hartford, Conn. Hartford: Press of the Case, Lockwood & Brainard Co., 1878-93. Reprint. New York: AMS Press, 1968.

Bristol

Bristol, Roger Pattrell. Supplement to Charles Evans' American bibliography. Charlottesville: Published for the Bibliographical Society of America and the Bibliographical Society of the University of Virginia [by] University Press of Virginia, 1970.

Brown, J.C. Cat., 1482-1700

Brown, John Carter. Bibliotheca Americana: a catalogue of books relating to North and South America in the library of the late John Carter Brown of Providence, R.I. Providence: Printed by H.O. Houghton and Co., Cambridge, 1875-82.

Brown, J.C. Cat., 1493-1800

Brown, John Carter. Bibliotheca Americana: a catalogue of books relating to North and South America in the library of John Carter Brown of Providence, R.I. Providence: Printed by H.O. Houghton and Co., Cambridge, 1865-71.

Brunet

Brunet, Jacques Charles. Manual de libraire et de l'amateur de livres. 5. éd., originale entièrement refondue et augm. d'un tiers par l'auteur ... Paris: Firmin Didot frères, fils et cie, 1860-65.
----- ----- Supplément. Par MM. P. Deschamps et G. Brunet. 1878-80.

BUCEM

The British union-catalog of early music printed before the year 1801: a record of the holdings of over one hundred libraries throughout the British Isles. Editor: Edith B. Schnapper. London: Butterworths Scientific Publications, 1957.

Buck, S.J. Travel

Buck, Solon Justus. Travel and description, 1765-1865, together with a list of county histories, atlases, and biographical collections and a list of territorial and state laws. Springfield, Ill.: The Trustees of the Illinois State Historical Library, 1914. Reprint. New York: B. Franklin, 1971.

Burndy. Science

Burndy Library, Norwalk, Conn. Heralds of science, as represented by two hundred epochal books and pamphlets selected from the Burndy Library. Norwalk, 1955. Reprint. Cambridge, Mass.: M.I.T. Press, 1969.

Caillet, A.L. Sciences psychiques

Caillet, Albert Louis. Manuel bibliographique des sciences psychiques ou occultes. Paris: L. Dorbon, 1912.

Cambridge. Sueltas

Cambridge. University. Library. Comedias sueltas in Cambridge University Library: a descriptive catalogue. Comp. by A.J.C. Bainton. Cambridge: University Library, 1977.

Campbell

Campbell, Marinus Frederik Andries Gerardus. Annales de la typographie néerlandaise au XV siècle. La Haye: M. Nijhoff, 1874.
----- ----- 1.-4. supplément. 1878-90.

Campbell-Kronenberg

Kronenberg, Maria Elizabeth. Campbell's Annales de la typographie néerlandaise au XV. siècle: contributions to a new edition. The Hague: M. Nijhoff, 1956.

Carter & Vervliet

Carter, Harry Graham, and Vervliet, Hendrik D.L. Civilité types. London:
Published for the Oxford Bibliographical Society by the Oxford U.P., 1966.

Carteret, L. Trésor, 1801-1875

Carteret, Léopold. Le trésor du bibliophile romantique et moderne, 1801-1875.
Par L. Carteret. Éd. rev., corr. et augm. Paris: L. Carteret, 1924-28.
Reprint. Paris: Editions du Vexin français, 1976.

Carteret, L. Trésor, 1875-1945

Carteret, Léopold. Le trésor du bibliophile: livres illustrés modernes, 1875
à 1945. Paris: L. Carteret, 1946-48.

Case, A.E. Poetical miscellanies

Case, Arthur Ellicott. A bibliography of English poetical miscellanies,
1521-1750. Oxford: Printed for the Bibliographical Society at the University Press, 1935 (for 1929). Reprint. Folcroft, Pa.: Folcroft Library Editions, 1970.

Checklist Amer. imprints

A Checklist of American imprints, 1830- . Metuchen, N.J.: Scarecrow Press, 1972-

Church, E.D. Discovery

Church, Elihu Dwight. A catalogue of books relating to the discovery and
early history of North and South America forming a part of the library of
E.D. Church. Comp. and annotated by George Watson Cole. New York: Dodd,
Mead and Co.; Cambridge: University Press, 1907.

Church, E.D. Engl. lit.

Church, Elihu Dwight. A catalogue of books, consisting of English literature
and miscellanea, including many original editions of Shakespeare, forming
a part of the library of E.D. Church. Comp. and annotated by George
Watson Cole. New York: Dodd, Mead and Co., 1909.

Cioranescu, A. 16. s.

Cioranescu, Alexandre. Bibliographie de la littérature française du seizième
siècle. Collaboration et préface de V.-L. Saulnier. Paris: C. Klinck-
sieck, 1959.

Cioranescu, A. 17. s.

Cioranescu, Alexandre. Bibliographie de la littérature française du dix-septième siècle. Paris: Editions du Centre national de la recherche scientifique, 1965-66.

Cioranescu, A. 18. s.

Cioranescu, Alexandre. Bibliographie de la littérature française du dix-huitième siècle. Paris: Editions du Centre national de la recherche scientifique, 1969.

Clark, T.D. Old South

Clark, Thomas Dionysius. Travels in the Old South: a bibliography. Norman: University of Oklahoma Press, 1956-59.

Cockle, M.J.D. Military books

Cockle, Maurice James Draffen. A bibliography of military books up to 1642 and of contemporary foreign works. London: Simpkin, Marshall, Hamilton, Kent, 1900. Reprint. "2nd ed." London: Holland Press, 1957.

Cockx-Indestege, E. Belgica typographica

Cockx-Indestege, Elly. Belgica typographica 1541-1600: catalogue librorum impressorum ab anno 1541 ad annum 1600 in regionibus quae nunc Regni Belgarum partes sunt. [Auctores] Elly Cockx-Indestege et Geneviève Glorieux. Nieuwkoop: B. de Graaf, 1968-

Cohen-De Ricci

Cohen, Henry. Guide de l'amateur de livres à gravures du XVIIIe siècle. 6. éd., rev., cor., et augm. par Seymour de Ricci. Paris: A. Rouquette, 1912.

Colas, R. Costume

Colas, René. Bibliographie générale du costume et de la mode. Paris: R. Colas, 1933. Reprint. New York: Hacker Books, 1963 & 1969.

Collins, D.C. News pamphlets

Collins, Douglas Cecil. A handlist of news pamphlets, 1590-1610. London: South-West Essex Technical College, 1943.

Copinger

Copinger, Walter Arthur. <u>Supplement to Hain's Repertorium bibliographicum.</u>
Berlin: J. Altmann, 1926. Reprint. Milano: Görlich, 1950.

Copinger-Reichling

Reichling, Dietrich. <u>Appendices ad Hainii-Copingeri Repertorium bibliographicum.</u> Munich: I. Rosenthal, 1905-11. Reprint. Milano: Görlich Editore, 1953.
----- ----- <u>Supplementum.</u> Monasterii Gvestphalorum: Theissingianis, 1914.

Cox, E.G. Travel

Cox, Edward Godfrey. <u>A reference guide to the literature of travel, including voyages, geographical descriptions, adventures, shipwrecks and expeditions.</u> Seattle: The University of Washington, 1935-49. Reprint. New York: Greenwood Press, 1969.

Craig, M.E. Scottish periodicals

Craig, Mary Elizabeth. <u>The Scottish periodical press, 1750-1789.</u> Edinburgh and London: Oliver and Boyd, 1931.

Crandall, M.L. Confederate imprints

Crandall, Marjorie Lyle. <u>Confederate imprints: a checklist based principally on the collections of the Boston Athenaeum.</u> Boston: Boston Athenaeum, 1955.

Crane & Kaye

Crane, Ronald Salmon, and Kaye, Frederick Benjamin. <u>A census of British newspapers and periodicals, 1620-1800.</u> Chapel Hill, N.C.: The University of North Carolina Press; London: Cambridge University Press, 1927.

Cranfield, G.A. Engl. provincial newspapers

Cranfield, Geoffrey Alan. <u>A hand-list of English provincial newspapers and periodicals, 1700-1760.</u> Cambridge: Bowes and Bowes, 1961.

Crawford, J.L.L. Cat. of printed books

Crawford, James Ludovic Lindsay, 26th Earl of. <u>Bibliotheca Lindesiana ... Catalogue of the printed books preserved at Haigh Hall, Wigan, co. pal. Lancast.</u> Aberdeen: Aberdeen University Press, 1910.

Crawford, J.L.L. Royal proclamations, 1485-1714

Crawford, James Ludovic Lindsay, 26th Earl of. A bibliography of royal pro-
     clamations of the Tudor and Stuart sovereigns and of others published
     under authority 1485-1714: with an historical essay on their origin and
     use. Bibliotheca Lindesiana. Oxford: Printed by the Clarendon Press,
     1910. Reprint. New York: B. Franklin, 1967.

Crawford, J.L.L. Royal proclamations, 1714-1910

Crawford, James Ludovic Lindsay, 26th Earl of. Handlist of proclamations
     issued by Royal and other constitutional authorities 1714-1910, George I
     to Edward VII, together with an index of names and places. Bibliotheca
     Lindesiana. Wigan: Roger and Rennick, 1913.

Currey, L.W. Science fiction

Currey, L.W. Science fiction and fantasy authors: a bibliography of first
     printings of their fiction and selected nonfiction. Boston: G.K. Hall,
     1979.

Dahl, F. Dutch corantos

Dahl, Folke. Dutch corantos, 1618-1650: a bibliography. The Hague: Konink-
     lijke Bibliotheek, 1946.

Dahl, F. Engl. corantos

Dahl, Folke. A bibliography of English corantos and periodical newsbooks,
     1620-1642. London: Bibliographical Society, 1952. Reprint. Boston:
     Longwood Press, 1977.

Darlow & Moule

British and Foreign Bible Society. Library. Historical catalogue of the
     printed editions of Holy Scripture in the Library of the British and
     Foreign Bible Society. Comp. by T.H. Darlow and H.F. Moule. London: The
     Bible House, 1903-11.

Day & Murray. Songbooks

Day, Cyrus Lawrence, and Murrie, Eleanore Boswell. English song-books, 1651-
     1702: a bibliography with a firstline index of songs. London: Printed
     for the Bibliographical Society at the University Press, Oxford, 1940.
     Reprints. Folcroft, Pa.: Folcroft Library Editions, 1975. Norwood, Pa.:
     Norwood Editions, 1976. Philadelphia: R. West, 1977.

Dean, B. Fishes

Dean, Bashford. A bibliography of fishes. New York: American Museum of Natural History, 1916-23. Reprint. New York: Russell & Russell, 1962.

Desgraves, L. Rép. 17. s.

Desgraves, Louis. Répertoire bibliographique des livres imprimés en France au XVIIe siècle. Baden-Baden: V. Koerner, 1978-

Deutsche Drucke des 16. Jh.

Bibliographie der deutschen Drucke des XVI. Jahrhunderts. Bad Bocklet: W. Krieg, 1960-

Dichter & Shapiro

Dichter, Harry, and Shapiro, Elliott. Early American sheet music, its lure and its lore, 1768-1889; including a directory of early American music publishers. New York: Bowker, 1941. Reprint, with corrections. New York: Dover Publications, 1977.

Drake, M. Almanacs

Drake, Milton. Almanacs of the United States. New York: Scarecrow Press, 1962.

Duff

Duff, Edward Gordon. Fifteenth century English books: a bibliography of books and documents printed in England and of books for the English market printed abroad. London: Printed for the Bibliographical Society at the Oxford University Press, 1917. Reprints. Folcroft, Pa.: Folcroft Library Editions, 1974. Norwood, Pa.: Norwood Editions, 1977. Philadelphia: R. West, 1978.

Duveen, D.I. Alchemica et chemica

Duveen, Denis I. Bibliotheca alchemica et chemica: an annotated catalogue of printed books on alchemy, chemistry and cognate subjects in the library of Denis I. Duveen. London: E. Weil, 1949.

Edelman, H.   Dutch-Amer. bib.

Edelman, Hendrik. <u>Dutch-American bibliography 1693-1794: a descriptive cata-</u>
<u>log of Dutch-language books, pamphlets and almanacs printed in America.</u>
Nieuwkoop: B. de Graaf, 1974.

Ellis Coll.

Kansas. University. Libraries. <u>A catalogue of the Ellis collection of orni-</u>
<u>thological books in the University of Kansas Libraries.</u> Comp. by
Robert M. Mengel. Lawrence, 1972-

Esdaile, A.J.K.   Tales

Esdaile, Arundell James Kennedy. <u>A list of English tales and prose romances</u>
<u>printed before 1740.</u> London: Printed for the Bibliographical Society by
Blades, East & Blades, 1912. Reprints. New York: B. Franklin, 1971.
Norwood, Pa.: Norwood Editions, 1973. Folcroft, Pa.: Folcroft Library
Editions, 1974. Philadelphia: R. West, 1977.

Estreicher

Estreicher, Karol Józef Teofil. <u>Bibliografia polska.</u> Kraków: W Druk. Uniw.
Jagiellońskiego. 1870-

Estreicher, K.J.T.   Bib. polska, 1881-1900

Estreicher, Karol Józef Teofil. <u>Bibliografia polska XIX stulecia: lata 1881-</u>
<u>1900.</u> Kraków: Nakł. Spółki Księgarzy Polskich, 1906-16.

Estreicher, K.J.T.   Bib. polska, 19. stulecia (Wyd. 2)

Estreicher, Karol Józef Teofil. <u>Bibliografia polska XIX stulecia.</u> Wyd. 2.
Kraków: Pánstwowe Wudawn. Naukowe, Oddział w Krakowie, 1959-

Evans

Evans, Charles. <u>American bibliography: a chronological dictionary of all</u>
<u>books, pamphlets, and periodical publications printed in the United</u>
<u>States of America from the genesis of printing in 1639 down to and in-</u>
<u>cluding the year 1820.</u> Chicago: Priv. print. for the author by the
Blakely Press, 1903-59. Reprints. New York: P. Smith, 1941-59. Metuchen, N.J.: Mini-Print Corp., 1967.

Faber du Faur

Yale University. Library. Yale Collection of German Literature. German Baroque literature: a catalogue of the collection in the Yale University Library. By Curt von Faber du Faur. New Haven: Yale University Press, 1958-69.

Ferguson, J. Bib. chemica

Glasgow. Royal College of Science and Technology. Andersonian Library. Bibliotheca chemica: a catalogue of the alchemical, chemical and pharmaceutical books in the collection of the late James Young. By John Ferguson. Glasgow: J. Maclehose and Sons, 1906. Reprint. London: Derek Verschoyle, Academic and Bibliographical Publications, 1954-

Ferguson, J.A. Australia

Ferguson, John Alexander. Bibliography of Australia. Sydney: Angus and Robertson, 1941-69. Reprint. Canberra: National Library of Australia, 1975-

Field, T.W. Indian bib.

Field, Thomas Warren. An essay towards an Indian bibliography: being a catalogue of books relating to the history, antiquities, languages, customs, religion, wars, literature, and origin of the American Indians, in the library of Thomas W. Field. New York: Scribner, Armstrong, and Co., 1873. Reprint. Detroit: Gale Research Co., 1967.

First printings of Amer. authors

First printings of American authors: contributions toward descriptive checklists. Matthew J. Bruccoli, series editor. Detroit: Gale Research Co., 1977-79.

Flake, C.J. Mormon bib.

Flake, Chad J. A Mormon bibliography, 1830-1930: books, pamphlets, periodicals, and broadsides relating to the first century of Mormonism. Salt Lake City: University of Utah Press, 1978.

Folger. Printed books

Folger Shakespeare Library. Catalog of printed books of the Folger Shakespeare Library, Washington, D.C. Boston: G.K. Hall, 1970.
-----First supplement. 1976.

Ford, W.C. Broadsides

Ford, Worthington Chauncey. <u>Broadsides, ballads, &c. printed in Massachusetts
1639-1800.</u> Boston: The Massachusetts Historical Society, 1922.

Fowler

Johns Hopkins University. John Work Garrett Library. <u>The Fowler architectural collection of Johns Hopkins University: catalogue.</u> Comp. by Lawrence Hall Fowler and Elizabeth Baer. Baltimore: Evergreen House Foundation, 1961.

Foxon

Foxon, David Fairweather. <u>English verse 1701-1750: a catalogue of separately
printed poems with notes on contemporary collected editions.</u> London and
New York: Cambridge University Press, 1975.

Frank, J. Engl. newspaper

Frank, Joseph. <u>The beginnings of the English newspaper, 1620-1660.</u> Cambridge, Mass.: Harvard University Press, 1961.

Franks bequest

British Museum. Dept. of Prints and Drawings. <u>Franks bequest: catalogue of
British and American book plates bequeathed to the Trustees of the
British Museum by Sir Augustus Wollaston Franks.</u> London: Printed by
order of the Trustees, 1903-04.

Freeman, R. Engl. emblem books

Freeman, Rosemary. <u>English emblem books.</u> London: Chatto & Windus, 1948.
Reprint. New York: Octagon Books, 1966.

Fuchs, G.F.C. Chemische Lit.

Fuchs, Georg Friedrich Christian. <u>Repertorium der chemischen Literatur von
494 vor Christi Geburt bis 1806 in chronol. Ordnung aufgestellt.</u> Hildesheim and New York: Olms, 1974.

Funck, M. Livre belge

Funck, M. <u>Le livre belge à gravures.</u> Paris and Brussels: C. Van Oest, 1925.

Gamba, B. Testi di lingua

  Gamba, Bartolommeo. <u>Serie dei testi di lingua.</u> 4. ed. Venice: Gondoliere,
      1839.

García Icazbalceta, J. Bib. mexicana (1954 ed.)

  García Icazbalceta, Joaquín. <u>Bibliografía mexicana del siglo XVI: catálogo</u>
      <u>razonado de libros impresos en México de 1539 a 1600.</u> Nueva ed., por
      Agustín Millares Carlo. México: Fondo de Cultura Económica, 1954.

Garrison-Morton (3rd ed.)

  Garrison, Fielding Hudson. <u>A medical bibliography (Garrison and Morton): an</u>
      <u>annotated check-list of texts illustrating the history of medicine.</u> By
      Leslie T. Morton. 3rd ed. Philadelphia: Lippincott, 1970.

Gartrell, E. Electricity

  Gartrell, Ellen. <u>Electricity, magnetism, and animal magnetism: a checklist of</u>
      <u>printed sources, 1600-1850.</u> Wilmington, Del.: Scholarly Resources, 1975.

George

  British Museum. Dept. of Prints and Drawings. <u>Catalogue of prints and draw-</u>
      <u>ings in the British Museum: Division I, political and personal satires.</u>
      Vols. 1-4 prepared by F.G. Stephens; v. 5-11 by M.D. George. London:
      Printed by order of the Trustees, 1870-1954. Reprint. London: Published
      for the Trustees of the British Museum by British Museum Publications
      Limited, 1978.

Gillett, C.R. McAlpin Coll.

  Gillett, Charles Ripley. <u>The McAlpin collection of British history and theol-</u>
      <u>ogy.</u> New York: Union Theological Seminary, 1924.

Goff

  Goff, Frederick R. <u>Incunabula in American libraries: a third census of fif-</u>
      <u>teenth-century books recorded in North American collections.</u> New York:
      Bibliographical Society of America, 1964. Reprint. Millwood, N.Y.:
      Kraus Reprint Co., 1973.
      ----- ----- <u>A supplement.</u> New York: Bibliographical Society of America,
      1972.

Goldsmiths' Lib. cat.

    London. University. Goldsmiths' Company's Library of Economic Literature. <u>Catalogue of the Goldsmiths' Library of Economic Literature.</u> Comp. by Margaret Canney and David Knott. London: Cambridge University Press, 1970-

Graff Coll.

    Newberry Library, Chicago. <u>A catalogue of the Everett D. Graff collection of Western Americana.</u> Comp. by Colton Storm. Chicago: Published for the Newberry Library by the University of Chicago Press, 1968.

Grüsse

    Grüsse, Johann Georg Theodor. <u>Trésor de livres rares et précieux.</u> Berlin: J. Altmann, 1922.

Greely, A.W.   First 14 congresses

    Greely, Adolphus Washington. <u>Public documents of the first fourteen con-gresses, 1789-1817: papers relating to early congressional documents.</u> Washington: Govt. Print. Off., 1900. Reprint. New York: Johnson Reprint Corp., 1973.
    ----- ----- <u>Supplement.</u> Washington: Govt. Print. Off., 1904.

Greg

    Greg, Walter Wilson. <u>A bibliography of the English printed drama to the Res-toration.</u> London: Printed for the Bibliographical Society at the University Press, Oxford, 1939-59. Reprint. London: Bibliographical Society, 1970.

Gregory

    United States. Library of Congress. <u>Catalogue of early books on music (be-fore 1800).</u> By Julia Gregory and Hazel Bartlett. Prepared under the direction of O.G. Sonneck. Washington: Govt. Print. Off., 1913. Reprint. New York: Da Capo Press, 1969.
    ----- ----- <u>Supplement.</u> (Books acquired by the Library 1913-1942.) By Hazel Bartlett. With a list of books on music in Chinese and Japanese. Washington, 1944.

Greswell, W.P.   Parisian Greek press

    Greswell, William Parr. <u>A view of the early Parisian Greek press.</u> Oxford: S. Collingwood, 1833.

Grolier. 100 Amer. books

Grolier Club, New York. One hundred influential American books printed before 1900: catalogue and addresses: exhibition at the Grolier Club, April eighteenth–June sixteenth, 1946. New York: The Grolier Club, 1947.

Grolier. 100 Engl. books

Grolier Club, New York. One hundred books famous in English literature, with facsimiles of the title pages and an introduction by George E. Woodberry. New York: The Grolier Club, 1902.

Grolier. Langland to Wither

Grolier Club, New York. Catalogue of original and early editions of some of the poetical and prose works of English writers from Langland to Wither. New York: Imprinted for the Cooper Square Publishers, 1963.

Grolier. Wither to Prior

Grolier Club, New York. Catalogue of original and early editions of some of the poetical and prose works of English writers from Wither to Prior. New York: Imprinted for the Cooper Square Publishers, 1963.

Gross, C. Brit. municipal history (2nd ed.)

Gross, Charles. A bibliography of British municipal history, including gilds and Parliamentary representation. 2nd ed. Leicester: Leicester University Press, 1966.

Guerra, F. Amer. medical bib.

Guerra, Francisco. American medical bibliography, 1639-1783. New York: L.C. Harper, 1962.

Gumuchian

Gumuchian et compagnie, booksellers, Paris. Les livres de l'enfance du XV. au XIX. siècle. Préface de Paul Gavault. Paris: En vente à la librairie Gumuchian & cie, [1931?]

GW

Gesamtkatalog der Wiegendrucke. Herausgegeben von der Kommission für den Gesamtkatalog der Wiegendrucke. Leipzig: K.W. Hiersemann, 1925- Reprint. Stuttgart: A. Hiersemann; New York: H.P. Krauss, 1968-

Haebler, K. Bib. ibérica

Haebler, Konrad. <u>Bibliografía ibérica del siglo XV.</u> The Hague and Leipzig: M.
Nijhoff, etc., 1903-17. Reprint. New York: B. Franklin, 1963.

Hagen, H.A. Bib. entomologica

Hagen, Hermann August. <u>Bibliotheca entomologica: die Literatur über das ganze
Gebiet der Entomologie bis zum Jahre 1862.</u> Leipzig: W. Engelmann, 1862-63.

Hain

Hain, Ludwig Friedrich Theodor. <u>Repertorium bibliographicum, in quo libri omnes ab
arte typographica inventa usque ad annum MD. typis expressi, ordine alphabe-
tico vel simpliciter enumeratur vel adcuratius recensentur.</u> Stuttgart: J.G.
Cotta, etc., 1826-38. Reprint. Milano: Görlich, 1948.

Hain-Copinger

Copinger, Walter Arthur. <u>Supplement to Hain's Repertorium bibliographicum.</u>
Berlin: J. Altmann, 1926. Reprint. Milano: Görlich, 1950.

Hain-Copinger-Reichling
Hain-Reichling

Reichling, Dietrich. <u>Appendices ad Hainii-Copingeri Repertorium bibliographicum.</u> Munich: I. Rosenthal, 1905-11. Reprint. Milano: Görlich Editore, 1953.
----- ----- <u>Supplementum.</u> Monasterii Gvestphalorum: Theissingianis, 1914.

Halkett & Laing (2nd ed.)

Halkett, Samuel, and Laing, John. <u>Dictionary of anonymous and pseudonymous English
literature.</u> New and enl. ed. Edinburgh: Oliver and Boyd, 1926-62.

Halkett & Laing (3rd ed.)

Halkett, Samuel, and Laing, John. <u>Dictionary of anonymous and pseudonymous publications in the English language.</u> 3rd ed. Harlow: Longman, 1980-

Hamilton, S. Amer. book illustrators (1968 ed.)

Princeton University. Library. <u>Early American book illustrators and wood
engravers, 1670-1870: a catalogue of a collection of American books,
illustrated for the most part with woodcuts and wood engravings, in the
Princeton Library.</u> With an introductory sketch by Sinclair Hamilton.
Princeton, N.J.: Princeton University Press, 1968.

Hammelmann, H.A.   Book illustrators 18th cent. England

Hammelmann, Hanns A.   Book illustrators in eighteenth-century England.   Ed.
    and completed by T.S.R. Boase.   New Haven: Published for the Paul Mellon
    Centre for Studies in British Art (London) by Yale University Press,
    1975.

Hanson

Hanson, Laurence William.   Comtemporary printed sources for British and Irish
    economic history, 1702-1750.   Cambridge: University Press, 1963.

Harrisse, H.   Americana

Harrisse, Henry.   Bibliotheca Americana vetustissima: a description of works
    relating to America, published between the years 1492 and 1551.   New
    York: G.P. Philes, 1866.
    ----- ----- Additions.   Paris: Tross; Leipzig: Imprimerie W. Drugulin,
    1872.

Harvard.   Architectural books

Harvard University.   Library.   Dept. of Printing and Graphic Arts.   Sixteenth-
    century architectural books from Italy and France: [exhibition] June-
    September 1971.   Cambridge, 1971.

Harwell, R.B.   Confederate imprints

Harwell, Richard Barksdale.   More Confederate imprints.   Richmond: Virginia
    State Library, 1957.

Hayward

National Book League, London.   English poetry: an illustrated catalogue of
    first and early editions, exhibited in 1947 at 7 Albemarle Street, Lon-
    don.   Comp. and rev. by John Hayward.   London: Cambridge Univ. Press,
    1950.   Reprint.   Westport, Conn.: Greenwood Press, 1975.

Heal, A.   Engl. writing-masters

Heal, Ambrose.   The English writing-masters and their copy-books, 1570-1880: a
    biographical dictionary & a bibliography, with an introduction on the
    development of handwriting by Stanley Morison.   Cambridge: University
    Press, 1931.

Heartman, C.F.   New England primer

Heartman, Charles Frederick. The New England primer issued prior to 1830: a bibliographical check-list for the more easy attaining the true knowledge of this book. New York: R.R. Bowker Co., 1934.

Heartman, C.F.   Non-New England primers

Heartman, Charles Frederick. American primers, Indian primers, Royal primers, and thirty-seven other types of non-New England primers issued prior to 1830: a bibliographical checklist. Highland Park, N.J.: Printed for H.B. Weiss, 1935.

Hebrew Union College.   Jewish Americana

Hebrew Union College-Jewish Institute of Religion. Library. Jewish Americana: a catalogue of books and articles ... found in the Library of the Hebrew Union College-Jewish Institute of Religion in Cincinnati: a supplement to A.S.W. Rosenbach: An American Jewish bibliography. Cincinnati: American Jewish Archives, 1954.

Heltzel, V.B.   Courtesy books in the Newberry

Newberry Library, Chicago. A check list of courtesy books in the Newberry library. Comp. by Virgil B. Heltzel. Chicago: The Newberry Library, 1942.

Henderson, R.W.   Amer. sport (3rd ed.)

Henderson, Robert William. Early American sport: a check-list of books by American and foreign authors published in America prior to 1860, including sporting songs. 3rd ed., rev. and enl. Rutherford: Farleigh Dickenson University Press, 1977.

Henrey, B.   Brit. botanical lit.

Henrey, Blanche. British botanical and horticultural literature before 1800. London and New York: Oxford University Press, 1975.

Herbert, A.S.   Engl. Bible

Herbert, Arthur Sumner. Historical catalogue of printed editions of the English Bible, 1525-1961. Rev. and expanded from the edition of T.H. Darlow and H.F. Moule, 1903. London: British & Foreign Bible Society; New York: The American Bible Society, 1968.

Hill, F.P. Amer. plays

Hill, Frank Pierce. American plays printed 1714-1830: a bibliographical record. Stanford University, Calif.: Stanford University Press; London: H.
Milford, Oxford University Press, 1934. Reprints. New York: B. Blom,
1968. New York: B. Franklin, 1970.

Hills, M.T. Engl. Bible in Amer.

Hills, Margaret Thorndike. The English Bible in America: a bibliography of
editions of the Bible & the New Testament published in America, 1777-
1957. Reprinted with corrections & revisions. New York: American
Bible Society, 1962.

Hispanic Society. Printed books, 1468-1700

Hispanic Society of America. Printed books, 1468-1700, in the Hispanic Society of America: a listing. By Clara Louisa Penney. New York, 1965.

Hitchcock, H.R. Amer. architectural books

Hitchcock, Henry Russell. American architectural books: a list of books,
portfolios, and pamphlets on architecture and related subjects published
in America before 1895. New expanded ed., with a new introd. by Adolf K.
Placzek; and included as an appendix: Chronological short-title list of
Henry-Russell Hitch[c]ock's American architectural books, comp. under
the direction of William H. Jordy, and A listing of architectural periodicals before 1895. New York: Da Capo Press, 1976.

Hoe, R. Auction cat.

Hoe, Robert. Catalogue of the library of Robert Hoe of New York: illuminated
manuscripts, incunabula, historical bindings, early English literature,
rare Americana, French illustrated books, eighteenth century English
authors, autographs, manuscripts, etc. ... To be sold by auction ... by
the Anderson Auction Co., New York. New York: D. Taylor & Co., 1911-
1912.

Horblitt, H.D. Grolier 100 science books

Horblit, Harrison D. One hundred books famous in science: based on an exhibition held at the Grolier Club. By Harrison D. Horblit. New York,
1964.

Hoskins, J.W. Polonica

Hoskins, Janina W. Early and rare Polonica of the 15th-17th centuries in
American libraries: a bibliographical survey. Boston: G.K. Hall, 1973.

Houzeau & Lancaster. Astronomie (1964 ed.)

Houzeau, Jean Charles, and Lancaster, A. Bibliographie générale de l'astronomie jusqu'en 1880. Nouv. éd., avec introd. et table des auteurs par D.W. Dewhirst. London: Holland Press, 1964.

Howes, W. U.S.iana (2nd ed.)

Howes, Wright. U.S.iana, 1650-1950: a selective bibliography in which are described 11,620 uncommon and significant books relating to the continental portion of the United States. Rev. and enl. [i.e. 2nd] ed. New York: Bowker for the Newberry Library, 1962. Reprint. New York: Bowker, 1978.

Hubach, R.R. Midwestern travel

Hubach, Robert Rogers. Early Midwestern travel narratives: an annotated bibliography, 1634-1850. Detroit: Wayne State University Press, 1961.

Hunt botanical cat.

Hunt, Rachel McMasters Miller. Catalogue of botanical books in the collection of Rachel McMasters Miller Hunt. Comp. by Jane Quinby. Pittsburgh: Hunt Botanical Library. 1958-61.

Huth, H. Auction cat.

Huth, Henry. Catalogue of the famous library of printed books, illuminated manucripts, autograph letters and engravings collected by Henry Huth, and since maintained and augmented by his son, Alfred H. Huth ... The printed books and illuminated manuscripts ... sold by auction by Messrs. Sotheby, Wilkinson & Hodge, auctioneers. London: Dryden Press, J. Davy and Sons, 1911-20.

IBP

Bohonos, Maria, and Szandorowska, Elisa. Incunabula quae in bibliothecis Poloniae asservantur. Wratislaviae: Ex Officina Instituti Ossoliniani, 1970.

IGI

Guarnaschelli, Teresa Maria, and Valenziani, E. Indice generale degli incunaboli delle biblioteche d'Italia. Roma: La Libreria dello stato, 1943-72.

Index Aureliensis

Index Aureliensis: catalogus librorum sedecimo saeculo impressorum. Aureliae
Aquensis, 1962-

Isaac

Isaac, Francis Swinton. An index to the early printed books in the British
Museum. Part II. MDI-MDXX. Section II. Italy. Section III. Switzer-
land and eastern Europe. London: Bernard Quaritch, 1938.

JCB Lib. cat., 1675-1700

Brown University. John Carter Brown Library. Bibliotheca Americana: catalogue of the John Carter Brown Library in Brown University, books printed
1675-1700. Providence: Brown University Press, 1973.

JCB Lib. cat., additions 1471-1700

Brown University. John Carter Brown Library. Bibliotheca Americana: catalogue of the John Carter Brown Library in Brown University, short-title
list of additions, books printed 1471-1700. Providence: Brown University
Press, 1973.

JCB Lib. cat., pre-1675

Brown University. John Carter Brown Library. Bibliotheca Americana: catalogue of the John Carter Brown Library in Brown University, Providence,
Rhode Island. Providence, 1919-31.

Johnson, M. de V. First editions (4th ed.)

Johnson, Merle de Vore. Merle Johnson's American first editions. 4th ed.,
rev. and enl. by Jacob Blanck. New York: Bowker, 1942. Reprint. Cambridge, Mass.: Research Classics, 1962.

Kaplan, L. Autobiographies

Kaplan, Louis. A bibliography of American autobiographies. Madison: University of Wisconsin Press, 1961.

Karpinski, L.C. Mathematical works

Karpinski, Louis Charles. Bibliography of mathematical works printed in America through 1850. Ann Arbor: The University of Michigan Press; London:
H. Milford, Oxford University Press, 1940.

Klebs

Klebs, Arnold Carl. Incunabula scientifica et medica: short title list.
Bruges: The Saint Catherine Press, 1938. Reprint. Hildesheim: G. Olms,
1963.

Knuttel

Hague. Koninklijke Bibliotheek. Catalogus van de pamfletten-verzameling
berustende in de Koninklijke Bibliotheek. Bewerkt door Dr. W.P.C.
Knuttel. 's Gravenhage: Algemeene Landsdrukkerij, 1889-1919.

Koeman, C. Atlantes Neerlandici

Koeman, Cornelis. Atlantes Neerlandici: bibliography of terrestrial, mari-
time, and celestial atlases and pilot books, published in the Netherlands
up to 1800. Amsterdam: Theatrum Orbis Terrarum, 1967-71.

Kress Lib.

Harvard University. Graduate School of Business Administration. Baker Library. Kress Library of Business and Economics. Catalogue: with data
upon cognate items in other Harvard libraries. Boston: Baker Library,
Harvard Graduate School of Business Administration, 1940-67.

Kronenberg

Kronenberg, Maria Elizabeth. Campbell's Annales de la typographie néerlandaise au XV. siècle: contributions to a new edition. The Hague: M.
Nijhoff, 1956.

Lancour, H. Art auction cats.

Lancour, Harold. American art auction catalogues, 1785-1942: a union list.
New York: New York Public Library, 1944.

Lande Coll.

McGill University, Montreal. Library. The Lawrence Lande collection of Cana-
diana in the Redpath Library of McGill University: a bibliography.
Collected, arranged, and annotated by Lawrence Lande. Montreal: Lawrence
Lande Foundation for Canadian Historical Research, 1965.
----- Rare and unusual Canadiana: first supplement to the Lande biblio-
graphy. Comp. by Lawrence Lande. Montreal: McGill University, 1971.

Landwehr, J. Dutch emblem books

Landwehr, John. <u>Dutch emblem books: a bibliography.</u> Utrecht: Haentjens Dekker & Gumbert, 1962.

Landwehr, J. Emblem books in the Low Countries

Landwehr, John. <u>Emblem books in the Low Countries, 1554-1949: a bibliography.</u>
Utrecht: Haentjens Dekker & Gumbert, 1970.

Landwehr, J. German emblem books

Landwehr, John. <u>German emblem books 1531-1888: a bibliography.</u> Utrecht:
Haentjens Dekker & Gumbert; Leiden: Sijthoff, 1972.

Lathem, E.C. Amer. newspapers

Lathem, Edward Connery. <u>Chronological tables of American newspapers, 1690-
1820.</u> Worcester, Mass.: American Antiquarian Society, 1972.

LC 18th cent. newspapers (1936 ed.)

United States. Library of Congress. Periodicals Division. <u>A check list of
American eighteenth century newspapers in the Library of Congress.</u> Originally comp. by John Van Ness Ingram. New ed., rev. and. enl. under the
direction of Henry S. Parsons. Washington: Govt. Print. Off., 1936.
Reprint. New York: Greenwood Press, 1968.

LC broadsides

United States. Library of Congress. Rare Book Division. <u>Catalog of broadsides in the Rare Book Division.</u> Boston: G.K. Hall, 1972.

LC children's books

United States. Library of Congress. Rare Book Division. <u>Children's books in
the Rare Book Division of the Library of Congress.</u> Totowa, N.J.: Rowman
and Littlefield, 1975.

LC coutumes

United States. Library of Congress. European Law Division. <u>The coutumes of
France in the Library of Congress: an annotated bibliography.</u> By Jean
Caswell and Ivan Sipkov. Washington: Library of Congress, 1977.

Leclerc, C. Bib. Americana

Leclerc, Charles. Bibliotheca Americana: histoire, géographie, voyages, archéologie et linguistique des deux Amériques et des îles Philippines. Paris: Maison-Neuve et cie, 1878.
----- ----- Supplément. n. 1, Novembre 1881-n. 2, 1881-87.

Legrand, E.L.J. Bib. hellénique 15.-16. s.

Legrand, Émile Louis Jean. Bibliographie hellénique, ou Description raisonnée des ouvrages publiés en grec par des Grecs au XVe et XVIe siècles. Paris: E. Leroux, 1885-1906. Reprint. Bruxelles: Culture et civilisation, 1963.

Legrand, E.L.J. Bib. hellénique 17. s.

Legrand, Émile Louis Jean. Bibliographie hellénique, ou Description raisonnée des ouvrages publiés par des Grecs au dix-septième siècle. Paris: A. Picard et fils, 1894-96; J. Maisonneuve, 1903. Reprints. New Rochelle, N.Y.: Caratzas, [1977?]. Bruxelles: Culture et civilisation, 1963.

Legrand, E.L.J. Bib. hellénique 18. s.

Legrand, Émile Louis Jean. Bibliographie hellénique, ou Description raisonnée des ouvrages publiés par des Grecs au dix-huitième siècle. Paris: Garnier frères, 1818-28. Reprints. New Rochelle, N.Y.: Caratzas, [1977?] Bruxelles: Culture et civilisation, 1963.

Lepper, G.M. Modern Amer. authors

Lepper, Gary M. A bibliographical introduction to seventy-five modern American authors. Berkeley, Calif.: Serendipity Books, 1976.

Lib. Company. Afro-Americana

Philadelphia. Library Company. Afro-Americana, 1553-1906: author catalog of the Library Company of Philadelphia and the Historical Society of Pennsylvania. Boston: G.K. Hall, 1973.

Lindsay & Neu. Mazarinades

Lindsay, Robert O., and Neu, John. Mazarinades: a checklist of copies in major collections in the United States. Metuchen, N.J.: Scarecrow Press, 1972.

Lipperheidesche Kostümbibliothek (2. Aufl.)

Berlin. Kunstbibliothek. <u>Katalog der Lipperheideschen Kostümbibliothek.</u>
Neubearbeitet von Eva Nienholdt und Gretel Wagner-Neumann. 2. völlig
neubearb. u. verm. Aufl. Berlin: Mann, 1965.

Lowens, I. Songsters

Lowens, Irving. <u>A bibliography of songsters printed in America before 1821.</u>
Worcester, Mass.: American Antiquarian Society, 1976.

Lowenstein, E. Amer. cookery (3rd ed.)

Lowenstein, Eleanor. <u>Bibliography of American cookery books, 1742-1860.</u> 3rd
ed. Worcester, Mass.: American Antiquarian Society, 1972.

Lowndes

Lowndes, William Thomas. <u>The bibliographer's manual of English literature,</u>
<u>containing an account of rare, curious, and useful books, published in or</u>
<u>relating to Great Britain and Ireland, from the invention of printing.</u>
New ed., rev., cor., and enl., with an appendix relating to the books of
literary and scientific societies, by Henry G. Bohn. London: G. Bell &
Sons, 1871. Reprint. Detroit: Gale Research Co., 1967.

MacLean, J.P. Shaker lit.

MacLean, John Patterson. <u>A bibliography of Shaker literature, with an intro-</u>
<u>ductory study of the writings and publications pertaining to Ohio be-</u>
<u>lievers.</u> Columbus: F.J. Heer, 1905. Reprint. New York: B. Franklin,
1971.

Maclean, V. Household and cookery books

Maclean, Virginia. <u>A short-title catalogue of household and cookery books</u>
<u>published in the English tongue 1701-1800.</u> London: Prospect; Charlottes-
ville, Va.: distributed by University Press of Virginia, 1981.

Madan

Madan, Falconer. <u>Oxford books: a bibliography of printed works relating to</u>
<u>the University and City of Oxford or printed or published there.</u> Oxford:
Clarendon Press, 1895-1931.

Madsen

Copenhagen. Kongelige Bibliotek. <u>Katalog over det Kongelige Biblioteks</u>
<u>inkunabler.</u> Ved Victor Madsen. København: Levin & Munksgaard,
1935-63.

Mahé, R. Livres de luxe

Mahé, Raymond. <u>Bibliographie des livres de luxe de 1900 à 1928 inclus.</u>
Paris: René Kieffer, 1931-43.

Marshall, R.G. STC Italian

<u>Short-title catalog of books printed in Italy and of books in Italian printed</u>
<u>abroad, 1501-1600, held in selected North American libraries.</u> Robert G.
Marshall, ed. Boston: G.K. Hall, 1970.

Martin, J. Privately printed books (2nd ed.)

Martin, John. <u>A bibliographical catalogue of privately printed books.</u> 2nd
ed. London, 1854. Reprint. New York: B. Franklin, 1970.

McAlpin Coll.

New York (City). Union Theological Seminary. Library. <u>Catalogue of the</u>
<u>McAlpin collection of British history and theology.</u> Comp. and ed. by
Charles Ripley Gillett. New York: Union Theological Seminary, 1927-30.

McBurney, W.H. Engl. prose fiction

McBurney, William Harlin. <u>A check list of English prose fiction, 1700-1739.</u>
Cambridge: Harvard University Press, 1960.

McCoy, R.E. Freedom

McCoy, Ralph Edward. <u>Freedom of the press: an annotated bibliography.</u> Carbondale: Southern Illinois University Press, 1968.
----- ----- <u>Ten-year supplement (1967-1977).</u> 1979.

McDade, T.M. Murder

McDade, Thomas M. <u>The annals of murder: a bibliography of books and pamphlets</u>
<u>on American murders from colonial times to 1900.</u> 1st ed. Norman: Uni-
versity of Oklahoma Press, 1961.

McKay, G.L. Amer. auction cats.

McKay, George Leslie. American book auction catalogues, 1713-1934: a union list. New York: The New York Public Library, 1937.

McLeod & McLeod. Anglo-Scottish tracts

McLeod, William Reynolds, and McLeod, V.B. Anglo-Scottish tracts, 1701-1714: a descriptive checklist. Lawrence: University of Kansas Libraries, 1979.

Mebane, J. Civil War

Mebane, John. Books relating to the Civil War: a priced check list, including regimental histories, Lincolniana, and Confederate imprints. New York: T. Yoseloff, 1963.

Medina, J.T. Bib. hispano-americana

Medina, José Toribio. Biblioteca hispano-americana (1493-1810). Santiago de Chile, 1898-1907. Reprint. Amsterdam: N. Israel, 1968.

Medina, J.T. Bib. hispano-chilena

Medina, José Toribio. Biblioteca hispano-chilena (1523-1817). Santiago de Chile: The author, 1897-99. Reprint. Amsterdam: N. Israel, 1965.

Medina, J.T. México

Medina, José Toribio. La imprenta en México (1539-1821). Santiago de Chile: The author, 1907-12. Reprint. Amsterdam: N. Israel, 1965.

Medina, J.T. Puebla de los Angeles

Medina, José Toribio. La imprenta en la Puebla de los Angeles (1640-1821). Santiago de Chile: Imprenta Cervantes, 1908. Reprint. Amsterdam: N. Israel, 1964.

Mendelssohn, S. South African bib.

Mendelssohn, Sidney. A South African bibliography to the year 1925 = 'N Suid-Afrikaanse bibliografie tot die Jaar 1925: being a revision and continuation of Sidney Mendelssohn's South African bibliography (1910). Ed. at the South African Library, Cape Town. London: Mansell, 1979.

Michel & Michel

Michel, Suzanne P., and Michel, Paul-Henri. Répertoire des ouvrages imprimés en langue italienne au XVIIe siècle. Firenze: L.S. Olschki, 1970-

Moraes, R.B. de. Bib. Brasiliana

Moraes, Rubens Borba de. Bibliographia Brasiliana: a bibliographical essay. Amsterdam: Colibris Editora, 1958.

Moraes, R.B. de. Bib. brasileira do período colonial

Moraes, Rubens Borba de. Bibliografia brasileira do período colonial. São Paulo: Instituto de Estudos Brasileiros, 1969.

Moreau

Moreau, Brigitte. Inventaire chronologique des éditions parisiennes du XVIe siècle ... d'après les manuscrits de Philippe Renouard. Paris: Imprimerie municipale, 1972-

Moreau, C. Mazarinades

Moreau, Célestin. Bibliographie des mazarinades. Paris: J. Renouard, 1850-51. Reprint. New York: B. Franklin, 1965.
----- [Supplements]. By Moreau, Van der Haeghen, Socard, and Labadie. 1859-1904.

Morgan

Morgan, William Thomas. A bibliography of British history (1700-1715) with special reference to the reign of Queen Anne. Bloomington, Ind., 1934-42. Reprint. New York: B. Franklin, 1972-73.

Mortimer, R. French 16th cent.

Harvard University. Library. Dept. of Printing and Graphic Arts. Catalogue of books and manuscripts. Pt. 1: French 16th century books. Comp. by Ruth Mortimer under the supervision of Philip Hofer and William A. Jackson. Pt. 2: Italian 16th century books. Comp. by Ruth Mortimer. Cambridge: Belknap Press of Harvard University Press, 1964-

Mortimer, R. Italian 16th cent.

Harvard University. Library. Dept. of Printing and Graphic Arts. Catalogue of books and manuscripts. Pt. 1: French 16th century books. Comp. by Ruth Mortimer under the supervision of Philip Hofer and William A. Jackson. Pt. 2: Italian 16th century books. Comp. by Ruth Mortimer. Cambridge: Belknap Press of Harvard University Press, 1964-

Mottelay, P.F. Electricity

Mottelay, Paul Fleury. Bibliographical history of electricity & magnetism, chronologically arranged. London: C. Griffin, 1922. Reprint. New York: Arno Press, 1975.

Muller, F. Amer.

Muller (Frederick) en Compagnie, Amsterdam. Catalogue of books, maps, plates on America and of a remarkable collection of early voyages. Amsterdam: F. Muller, 1872-75. Reprint. Amsterdam: N. Israel, 1966.

Munby & Coral

Munby, Alan Noel Latimer, and Coral, Lenore. British book sale catalogues, 1676-1800: a union list. London: Mansell, 1977.

Murray, C.F. French books

Murray, Charles Fairfax. Catalogue of a collection of early French books in the library of C. Fairfax Murray. Comp. by Hugh Wm. Davies. London: Priv. print., 1910.

Murray, C.F. German books

Murray, Charles Fairfax. Catalogue of a collection of early German books in the library of C. Fairfax Murray. Comp. by Hugh Wm. Davies. London: Priv. print., 1913.

NCBEL

New Cambridge bibliography of English literature. Ed. by George Watson. Cambridge: University Press, 1969-77.

New Sabin

Thompson, Lawrence Sidney. <u>The new Sabin: books described by Joseph Sabin and
his successors, now described again on the basis of examination of originals, and fully indexed by title, subject, joint authors, and institutions and agencies.</u> Troy, N.Y.: Whitston Pub. Co., 1974-

Nielsen, L.M. Dansk bib.

Nielsen, Lauritz Martin. <u>Dansk bibliografi, 1482-1600 med saerligt hensyn til
dansk bogtrykkerkunsts historie.</u> København: Gyldendal, 1919-33.

Nijhoff & Kronenberg

Nijhoff, Wouter, and Kronenberg, Maria Elizabeth. <u>Nederlandsche bibliographie
van 1500 tot 1540.</u> 's-Gravenhage: M. Nijhoff, 1923-1971.

Nissen, C. Botanische Buchillustration (2. Aufl.)

Nissen, Claus. <u>Die botanische Buchillustration: ihre Geschichte und Bibliographie.</u> 2. Aufl., durchgesehener und verb. Abdruck der zweibändigen
Erstaufl., ergänzt durch ein Supplement. Stuttgart: Hiersemann, 1966.

Nissen, C. Illustrierte Vogelbücher

Nissen, Claus. <u>Die illustrierten Vogelbücher: ihre Geschichte und Bibliographie.</u> Stuttgart: Hiersemann Verlag, 1953. Reprint. Stuttgart:
Hiersemann Verlag, 1976.

Nissen, C. Schöne Fischbücher

Nissen, Claus. <u>Schöne Fischbücher: kurze Geschichte der ichthyologischen
Illustration: Bibliographie fischkundlicher Abbildungswerke.</u> Stuttgart:
L. Hempe Verlag, 1951.

Nissen, C. Schöne Vogelbücher

Nissen, Claus. <u>Schöne Vogelbücher: ein Überblick der ornithologischen Illustration, nebst Bibliographie.</u> Wien, etc.: H. Reichner, 1936.

Nissen, C. Zoologische Buchillustration

Nissen, Claus. <u>Die zoologische Buchillustration: ihre Bibliographie und
Geschichte.</u> Stuttgart: Hiersemann, 1966-

NLM 16th cent.

United States. National Library of Medicine. A catalogue of sixteenth century printed books in the National Library of Medicine. Comp. by Richard J. Durling. Bethesda, Md., 1967.

Norton, F.J. Italian printers

Norton, Frederick John. Italian printers, 1501-1520: an annotated list with an introduction. London: Bowes and Bowes, 1958.

Norton, F.J. Spain and Portugal

Norton, Frederick John. A descriptive catalogue of printing in Spain and Portugal, 1501-1520. Cambridge and New York: Cambridge University Press, 1978.

NUC

National union catalog: a cumulative author list representing Library of Congress printed cards and titles reported by other American libraries. Washington: Library of Congress, 1956-

NUC pre-1956

National union catalog, pre-1956 imprints: a cumulative author list representing Library of Congress printed cards and titles reported by other American libraries. London: Mansell, 1968-1980.
----- Supplement. 1980-1981.

Oates

Cambridge. University. Library. A catalogue of the fifteenth-century printed books in the University Library, Cambridge. Comp. by J.C.T. Oates. Cambridge: University Press, 1954.

Olivier, E. Reliures armoriées

Olivier, Eugène; Hermal, Georges; and Roton, R. de. Manuel de l'amateur de reliures armoriées françaises. Paris: C. Bosse, 1924-35.

Osborne Coll.

Toronto. Public Libraries. Boys and Girls Services. The Osborne collection of early children's books: a catalogue prepared at Boys and Girls House. By Judith St. John. Toronto: Toronto Public Library, 1958-75.

Osler, W. Bib. Osleriana

Osler, William. Bibliotheca Osleriana: a catalogue of books illustrating the history of medicine and science, collected, arranged and annotated by Sir William Osler and bequeathed to McGill University. Oxford: Clarendon Press, 1929. Reprint. Montreal: McGill-Queen's University Press, 1969.

Palau y Dulcet

Palau y Dulcet, Antonio. Manual del librero hispano-americano: inventario bibliográfico de la producción científica y literaria de España y de la América latina desde la invención de la imprenta hasta nuestros días, con el valor comercial de todos los artículos descritos. Barcelona: Librería anticuaria, 1923-27.

Palau y Dulcet (2nd ed.)

Palau y Dulcet, Antonio. Manual del librero hispano-americano: bibliografía general española e hispano-americana desde la invención de la imprenta hasta nuestros tiempos, con el valor comercial de los impresos descritos. 2. ed. corr. y aumentada por el autor. Barcelona: A. Palau, 1948-77.

Palmer, P.M. German works on Amer.

Palmer, Philip Motley. German works on America, 1492-1800. Berkeley: University of California Press, 1952.

Panzer

Panzer, Georg Wolfgang Franz. Annales typographici ab artis inventae origine ad annum MD. Nuremburg: J.B. Zeh, 1793-1803.

Paris. Université. Cat., 1501-1540

Paris. Université. Bibliothèque. Catalogue de la réserve XVIe siècle (1501-1540) de la bibliothèque de l'Université de Paris. Par Charles Beaulieux. Paris: H. Champion, 1910. Reprint. New York: B. Franklin, 1969.
----- ----- Supplément et suite (1541-1550). 1923.

Parsons, W.   Catholic Americana

Parsons, Wilfrid. Early Catholic Americana: a list of books and other works by Catholic authors in the United States, 1729-1830. New York: Macmillan, 1939. Reprints. Boston: Milford House, 1973. Boston: Longwood Press, 1977.
----- List of additions and corrections to Early Catholic Americana.
Contribution of French translations (1724-1820) by Forrest Bowe. New York: Franco-Americana, 1952.

Pellechet

Pellechet, Marie Léontine Catherine. Catalogue général des incunables des bibliothèques publiques de France. Paris: A. Picard, 1897-1909. Reprint. Nendeln, Liechtenstein: Kraus-Thomson Organization Ltd., 1970.

Perrins, C.W.D.   Italian books

Perrins, Charles William Dyson. Italian book-illustrations and early printing: a catalogue of early Italian books in the library of C.W. Dyson Perrins. Oxford: University Press, etc., 1914.

Pforzheimer

Pforzheimer, Carl Howard. The Carl H. Pforzheimer library: English literature, 1475-1700. New York: Priv. print., The Morrill Press, 1940.

Phillips

United States. Library of Congress. Map Division. A list of geographical atlases in the Library of Congress, with bibliographical notes. Vols. 1-4 comp. under the direction of P.L. Phillips. Washington: Govt. Print. Off., 1909- . Reprint (vols. 1-4). Amsterdam: Theatrum Orbis Terrarum, 1971.

Pia, P.   Livres de l'Enfer

Pia, Pascal. Les Livres de l'Enfer: bibliographie critique des ouvrages érotiques dans leurs différentes éditions du XVIe siècle à nos jours. Paris: C. Coulet et A. Faure, 1978.

PMM

Carter, John, and Muir, Percy H. Printing and the mind of man: a descriptive catalogue illustrating the impact of print on the evolution of Western civilization during five centuries. London: Cassell; New York: Holt Rinehart & Winston, 1967.

Polain

Polain, Louis. <u>Catalogue des livres imprimés au quinzième siècle des bibliothèques de Belgique.</u> Bruxelles: Pour la Société des bibliophiles & icon-
ophiles de Belgique, 1932.

Praet, J.B.B. van. Vélin, bib. du roi

Praet, Joseph Basile Bernard van. <u>Catalogue des livres imprimés sur vélin de
la bibliothèque de roi.</u> Paris: De Bure frères, 1822-28. Reprint. New
York: B. Franklin, 1965.

Praet, J.B.B. van. Vélin, bib. publiques

Praet, Joseph Basile Bernard van. <u>Catalogue des livres imprimés sur vélin,
qui se trouvent dans des bibliothèques tant publiques que particulières.</u>
Paris: De Bure frères, 1824-28. Reprint. New York: B. Franklin, 1965.

Pritzel

Pritzel, Georg August. <u>Thesaurus literaturae botanicae omnium gentium.</u> Leipzig: F.Z. Brockhaus, 1872-77. Reprint. Milano: Görlich, 1950.

Proctor

Proctor, Robert George Collier. <u>An index to the early printed books in the
British Museum.</u> London: Kegan Paul, Trench, Trübner, 1898-1903.

Quérard

Quérard, Joseph-Marie. <u>La France littéraire.</u> Paris: Didot père et fils,
1827-64. Reprint. Paris: Maisonneuve and Larose, 1964.

Rader, J.L. South of forty

Rader, Jesse Lee. <u>South of forty, from the Mississippi to the Rio Grande: a
bibliography.</u> 1st ed. Norman: University of Oklahoma Press, 1947.

Ransom, W. Private presses

Ransom, Will. <u>Private presses and their books.</u> New York: R.R. Bowker Co.,
1929. Reprint. New York: AMS Press, 1976.

Ray, G.N. Illustrator and the book in England

Ray, Gordon Norton. The illustrator and the book in England from 1790 to
    1914. New York: Pierpont Morgan Library, 1976.

Reginald, R. Science fiction

Reginald, R. Science fiction and fantasy literature: a checklist, 1700-1974:
    with Contemporary science fiction authors II. Detroit: Gale Research
    Co., 1979.

Reichling

Reichling, Dietrich. Appendices ad Hainii-Copingeri Repertorium bibliogra-
    phicum. Munich: I. Rosenthal, 1905-11. Reprint. Milano: Görlich Edi-
    tore, 1953.
----- ----- Supplementum. Monasterii Gvestphalorum: Theissingianis,
    1914.

Rép. 16. s.

Répertoire bibliographique des livres imprimés en France au seizième siècle.
    Baden-Baden: Librairie Heitz: Editions Valentin Koerner, 1968-

RISM

International inventory of musical sources = Répertoire international des
    sources musicales. München, etc.: G. Henle, etc., 1960-

Riccardi, P. Bib. matematica

Riccardi, Pietro. Biblioteca matematica italiana dalla origine della stampa
    ai primi anni del secolo XIX. Modena: Società tipografica, 1873-93.
----- Correzioni ed aggiunte, serie VII. Modena: Società tipografica
    modense, 1928. Reprint. Milano: Görlich, 1952.

Rink, E. Technical Americana

Rink, Evald. Technical Americana: a checklist of technical publications
    printed before 1831. Millwood, N.Y.: Kraus International Publications,
    1981.

Ritter, F.   Incun. alsaciens de la Bib. nat. de Strasbourg

Strasbourg. Bibliothèque nationale et universitaire. Catalogue des incunables alsaciens de la Bibliothèque nationale et universitaire de Strasbourg. Répertoire bibliographique des livres imprimés en Alsace au 16me
siècle, fascicules hors sér. I-V. Par François Ritter. Strasbourg:
Heitz, 1938.

Ritter, F.   Incun. de la Bib. municipale de Strasbourg

Strasbourg. Bibliothèque de la ville. Catalogue des incunables et livres du
XVIe siècle de la Bibliothèque municipale de Strasbourg. Par François
Ritter. Strasbourg: P.H. Heitz, 1948.

Ritter, F.   Incun. ne figurant pas à la Bib. nat. de Strasbourg

Ritter, François. Catalogue des incunables ne figurant pas à la Bibliothèque
nationale et universitaire de Strasbourg. Répertoire bibliographique des
livres imprimés en Alsace aux XVe et XVIe siècles, 3. ptie. Strasbourg:
P.H. Heitz, 1960.

Ritter, F.   Livres du 16. s. à la Bib. nat. de Strasbourg

Strasbourg. Bibliothèque nationale et universitaire. Répertoire bibliographique des livres du XVIe siècle qui se trouvent a la Bibliothèque nationale et universitaire de Strasbourg. Par F. Ritter. Strasbourg: P.H.
Heitz, 1937-55. Reprint. Naarden: A.W. v. Bekhoven, [1968?]

Ritter, F.   Livres du 16. s. ne figurant pas à la Bib. nat. de Strasbourg

Ritter, François. Catalogue des livres du XVIe siècle ne figurant pas à la
Bibliothèque nationale et universitaire de Strasbourg. Répertoire bibliographique des livres imprimés en Alsace aux XVe et XVIe siècles, 4.
ptie. Strasbourg: P.H. Heitz, 1960.

Rochedieu, C.A.E.   French translations

Rochedieu, Charles Alfred Emmanuel. Bibliography of French translations of
English works, 1700-1800. Chicago: University of Chicago Press, 1948.

Romaine, L.B.   Amer. trade cats.

Romaine, Lawrence B. A guide to American trade catalogs, 1744-1900. New
York: R.R. Bowker, 1960. Reprint. New York: Arno Press, 1976.

Ronalds, F. Electricity

Ronalds, Francis. Catalogue of books and papers relating to electricity, magnetism, the electric telegraph, &c., including the Ronalds Library. London and New York: E. & F.N. Spon, 1880.

Rosenbach, A.S.W. Amer. Jewish bib.

Rosenbach, Abraham Simon Wolf. An American Jewish bibliography: being a list of books and pamphlets by Jews, or relating to them, printed in the United States from the establishment of the press in the colonies until 1850. Baltimore: American Jewish Historical Society, 1926.

Rosenbach, A.S.W. Children's books

Rosenbach, Abraham Simon Wolf. Early American children's books, with bibliographical descriptions of the books in his private collection. Portland, Me.: The Southworth Press, 1933. Reprints. New York: Kraus Reprint Corp., 1966. New York: Dover Publications, 1971.

Rosenwald

United States. Library of Congress. A catalog of the gifts of Lessing J. Rosenwald to the Library of Congress, 1943 to 1975. Washington: Library of Congress, 1977.

Rothschild

Rothschild, Nathaniel Mayer Victor. The Rothschild library: a catalogue of the collection of eighteenth-century printed books and manuscripts formed by Lord Rothschild. Cambridge [Eng.]: Priv. print. at the University Press, 1954.

Rothschild, N.J.E. Cat.

Rothschild, Nathan James Edouard. Catalogue des livres composant la bibliothèque de feu M. la baron James de Rothschild. Paris: D. Morgand, 1884-1920.

Rowlands, W. Cambrian bib.

Rowlands, William. Cambrian bibliography: containing an account of the books printed in the Welsh language, or relating to Wales, from the year 1546 to the end of the eighteenth century, with biographical notices. Ed. and enl. by the Rev. D. Silvan Evans. Llanidloes: Print. and pub. by J. Pryse, 1869. Reprint. Amsterdam: Meridian Pub. Co., 1970.

Sabin

Sabin, Joseph. <u>A dictionary of books relating to America, from its discovery</u>
<u>to the present time.</u> New York, 1868-1936. Reprints. New York: Mini-
Print Corp., 196-? Metuchen, N.J.: Scarecrow Press, 1966.

Sadleir, M. 19th cent. fiction

Sadleir, Michael. <u>XIX century fiction: a bibliographical record based on his</u>
<u>own collection.</u> London: Constable; Berkeley: University of California
Press, 1951. Reprint. New York: Cooper Square Publishers, 1969.

Sander

Sander, Max. <u>Le livre à figures italien depuis 1467 jusqu'à 1530: essai de sa</u>
<u>bibliographie et de son histoire.</u> New York: G.E. Stechert, 1941 [i.e.
1941-43]
----- <u>Supplément.</u> By Carlo Enrico Rava. Milan: U. Hoepli, 1969.

Saricks, A. Melvin Coll.

Saricks, Ambrose. <u>A bibliography of the Frank E. Melvin collection of pam-</u>
<u>phlets of the French Revolution in the University of Kansas Libraries.</u>
Lawrence: University of Kansas Libraries, 1960.

Sayle

Cambridge. University. Library. <u>Early English printed books in the Uni-</u>
<u>versity Library, Cambridge (1475-1640).</u> Comp. by Charles Edward Sayle.
Cambridge: University Press, 1900-07. Reprint. New York: Johnson
Reprint Corp., 1971.

Schreiber, W.L. Handbuch (3. Aufl.)

Schreiber, Wilhelm Ludwig. <u>Handbuch der Holz- und Metallschnitte des XV.</u>
<u>Jahrhunderts = Manuel de l'amateur de la gravure sur bois et sur metal au</u>
<u>XVe siècle.</u> 3. Aufl. Vollständiger Neudruck des Gesamtwerkes. Stutt-
gart: A. Hiersemann; Nendeln: Kraus Reprint, 1969.

Schwerdt, C.F.G.R. Hunting

Schwerdt, Charles Francis George Richard. <u>Hunting, hawking, shooting, illus-</u><u>trated in a catalogue of books, manuscripts, prints, and drawings, col-</u><u>lected by C.F.G.R. Schwerdt.</u> London: Priv. print. for the author by Waterlow & Sons ltd., 1928-37.

Seidensticker, O. German printing

Seidensticker, Oswald. <u>The first century of German printing in America,</u><u>1728-1830.</u> Philadelphia: Schaefer & Koradi, 1893. Reprints. New York: Kraus Reprint Corp., 1966. Millwood, N.Y.: Kraus Reprint, 1980.
----- <u>A new supplement.</u> By Gerhard Friedrich. Philadelphia, 1940.

Shaaber, M.A. 16th cent. imprints

Pennsylvania. University. Libraries. <u>Sixteenth-century imprints in the</u><u>libraries of the University of Pennsylvania.</u> By M.A. Shaaber. Phila-delphia: University of Pennsylvania Press, 1976.

Shaaber, M.A. Brit. authors

Shaaber, Matthias Adam. <u>Check-list of works of British authors printed</u><u>abroad, in languages other than English, to 1641.</u> New York: Biblio-graphical Society of America, 1975.

Shaw & Shoemaker

Shaw, Ralph Robert, and Shoemaker, Richard H. <u>American bibliography: a pre-</u><u>liminary checklist for 1801-1819.</u> New York: Scarecrow Press, 1958-66.

Shipton & Mooney

Shipton, Clifford Kenyon, and Mooney, James E. <u>National index of American</u><u>imprints throught 1800: the short-title Evans.</u> Worcester, Mass.: Ameri-can Antiquarian Society, 1969.

Shoemaker

Shoemaker, Richard H. <u>A checklist of American imprints for 1820-1829.</u> New York: Scarecrow Press, 1964-71.

Silva, I.F. da. Diccionário bib. portuguez

Silva, Innocencio Francisco da. <u>Diccionário bibliográphico portuguez.</u> Lisboa: Na Imprensa nacional, 1858-1923.

Simon, A.L. Bib. gastronomica

Simon, André Louis. <u>Bibliotheca gastronomica: a catalogue of books and documents on gastronomy: the production, taxation, distribution and consumption of food and drink, their use and abuse in all times and among all peoples.</u> London: Wine and Food Society, 1953.

Smith, C.W. Pacific Northwest (3rd ed.)

Smith, Charles Wesley. <u>Pacific Northwest Americana: a check list of books and pamphlets relating to the history of the Pacific Northwest.</u> 3rd ed., rev. and extended by Isabel Mayhew. Portland, Or.: Binfords & Mort, 1950.

Smith, D.E. Rara arithmetica (4th ed.)

Smith, David Eugene. <u>Rara arithmetica: a catalogue of the arithmetics written before the year MDCI with a description of those in the library of George Arthur Plimpton of New York.</u> 4th ed. New York: Chelsea Publ. Co., 1970.

Smith, J. Anti-Quakeriana

Smith, Joseph, bookseller. <u>Bibliotheca anti-Quakeriana, or, A catalogue of books adverse to the Society of Friends, alphabetically arranged, with biographical notices of the authors.</u> London: J. Smith, 1873. Reprint. New York: Kraus Reprint Co., 1968.

Smith, J. Friends' books

Smith, Joseph, bookseller. <u>A descriptive catalogue of Friends' books, or books written by members of the Society of Friends, commonly called Quakers, from their first rise to the present time, interspersed with critical remarks and ... biographical notices.</u> London: J. Smith, 1867. ----- <u>Supplement.</u> London: E. Hicks, 1893.

Sonneck, O.G.T. Librettos

United States. Library of Congress. Music Division. <u>Catalogue of opera librettos printed before 1800.</u> Prepared by Oscar George Theodore Sonneck. Washington: Govt. Print. Off., 1914. Reprint. New York: B. Franklin, 1967.

Sonneck-Upton

Sonneck, Oscar George Theodore. <u>A bibliography of early secular American music (18th century).</u> Rev. and enl. by William Treat Upton. Washington: The Library of Congress, Music Division, 1945. Reprint. New York: Da Capo Press, 1964.

Spear, D.N. Amer. directories

Spear, Dorothea N. <u>Bibliography of American directories through 1860.</u> Worcester, Mass.: American Antiquarian Society, 1961. Reprint. Westport, Conn.: Greenwood Press, 1978.

Spielmann, P.E. Miniature books

Spielmann, Percy Edwin. <u>Catalogue of the library of miniature books collected by Percy Edwin Spielmann.</u> London: E. Arnold, 1961.

STC

Pollard, Alfred William, and Redgrave, G.R. <u>A short-title catalogue of books printed in England, Scotland & Ireland and of English books printed abroad, 1475-1640.</u> London: Bibliographical Society, 1926. Reprint. London: Bibliographical Society, 1969.

STC (2nd ed.)

Pollard, Alfred William, and Redgrave, G.R. <u>A short-title catalogue of books printed in England, Scotland & Ireland and of English books printed abroad, 1475-1640.</u> 2nd ed., rev. & enl., begun by W.A. Jackson & F.S. Ferguson, completed by Katharine F. Pantzer. London: Bibliographical Society, 1976-

Starnes, D.T. Renaissance dictionaries

Starnes, De Witt Talmage. <u>Renaissance dictionaries, English-Latin and Latin-English.</u> Austin: University of Texas Press, 1954.

Starr, E.C. Baptist bib.

Starr, Edward Caryl. <u>A Baptist bibliography, being a register of printed material by and about Baptists: including works written against the Baptists.</u> Philadelphia, etc.: Published by the Judson Press for the Samuel Colgate Baptist Historical Collection, Colgate University, etc., 1947-76.

Stewart, P. Brit. newspapers

Stewart, Powell. British newspapers and periodicals, 1632-1800: a descriptive catalogue of a collection at the University of Texas. Austin: University of Texas, 1950.

Stillwell, M.B. Science

Stillwell, Margaret Bingham. The awakening interest in science during the first century of printing, 1450-1550: an annotated checklist of first editions viewed from the angle of their subject content. New York: Bibliographical Society of America, 1970.

Stillwell, M.B. World of books, 1450-1470

Stillwell, Margaret Bingham. The beginning of the world of books, 1450-1470: a chronological survey of the texts chosen for printing during the first twenty years of the printing arts, with a synopsis of the Gutenberg documents. New York: Bibliographical Society of America, 1972.

Stoddard, R.E. Unrecorded Wegelin

Stoddard, Roger Eliot. A catalogue of books and pamphlets unrecorded in Oscar Wegelin's Early American poetry, 1650-1820. Providence, R.I.: Friends of the Library of Brown University, 1969.

Stratman, C.J. Engl. printed tragedy

Stratman, Carl Joseph. Bibliography of English printed tragedy, 1565-1900. Carbondale: Southern Illinois University Press, 1966.

Streeter Americana

Parke-Bernet Galleries, inc., New York. The celebrated collection of Americana formed by the late Thomas Winthrop Streeter. New York, 1966-69.

Summers, M. Gothic bib.

Summers, Montague. A Gothic bibliography. London: The Fortune Press, 1941. Reprint. London: Fortune Press, 1969.

Sveriges bib.

Sveriges bibliografi 1481-1600. Uppsala: Svenska litteratursällskapet, 1927-33.

Talvart & Place. Auteurs modernes

Talvart, Hector, and Place, Joseph. <u>Bibliographie des auteurs modernes de langue française.</u> Paris: Éditions de la Chronique des lettres françaises, 1928-76.

Tchemerzine

Tchemerzine, Avenir. <u>Bibliographie d'éditions originales et rares d'auteurs français des XVe, XVIe, XVIIe, et XVIIIe siècles.</u> Paris: Plée, 1927-34. Reprints. Teaneck [N.J.]: Somerset House, 1973. Paris: Hermann, 1977.

Thomason Coll.

British Museum. Dept. of Printed Books. Thomason Collection. <u>Catalogue of the pamphlets, books, newspapers, and manuscripts relating to the Civil War, the Commonwealth, and Restoration, collected by George Thomason, 1640-1661.</u> London: Printed by order of the Trustees, 1908.

Thompson, R. Annuals

Thompson, Ralph. <u>American literary annuals & gift books, 1825-1865.</u> New York: H.W. Wilson Co., 1936. Reprint. Hamden, Conn.: Archon Books, 1967.

Thomson, T.R. Railroads

Thomson, Thomas Richard. <u>Check list of publications on American railroads before 1841: a union list of printed books and pamphlets, including state and federal documents, dealing with charters, by-laws, legislative acts, speeches, debates, land grants, officers' and engineers' reports, travel guides, maps, etc.</u> New York: The New York Public Library, 1942.

Tiele, P.A. Journaux navigateurs

Tiele, Pieter Anton. <u>Mémoire bibliographique sur les journaux navigateurs néerlandais réimprimés dans les collections de De Bry et de Hulsius et dans les collections hollandaises du XVIIe siècle, et sur les anciennes éditions hollandaises des journaux de navigateurs étrangers, la plupart en la possession de Frédérik Muller à Amsterdam.</u> Amsterdam: F. Muller, 1867. Reprint. Amsterdam: N. Israel, 1960.

Times handlist

The Times, London. <u>Tercentenary handlist of English & Welsh newspapers, magazines & reviews.</u> London: The Times, 1920.

Tinker lib.

Tinker, Chauncey Brewster. The Tinker library: a bibliographical catalogue of the books and manuscripts collected by Chauncey Brewster Tinker. Comp. by Robert F. Metzdorf. New Haven: Yale University Library, 1959.

Tissandier, G. Bib. aéronautique

Tissandier, Gaston. Bibliographie aéronautique: catalogue de livres d'histoire, de science, de voyages et de fantaisie, traitant de la navigation aérienne ou des aérostats. Paris: H. Launette et cie, 1887.

Tomkinson, G.S. Modern presses

Tomkinson, Geoffrey Stewart. A select bibliography of the principal modern presses, public and private, in Great Britain and Ireland. London: First Edition Club, 1928. Reprint. San Francisco: A. Wofsy Fine Arts, 1975.

Toole-Stott, R. Conjuring

Toole-Stott, Raymond. A bibliography of English conjuring. Derby: Harper and Sons, 1976-78.

Tooley, R.V. Coloured plates (1979 ed.)

Tooley, Ronald Vere. English books with coloured plates, 1790-1860: a bibliographical account of the most important books illustrated by English artists in colour aquatint and colour lithography. Rev. ed. Folkestone, Eng.: Dawson, 1979.

Tremaine

Tremaine, Marie. A bibliography of Canadian imprints, 1751-1800. Toronto: University of Toronto Press, 1952.

Vicaire, G. Bib. gastronomique

Vicaire, Georges. Bibliographie gastronomique. Paris: P. Rouquette et fils, 1890.

Vicaire, G. Livres du 19. s.

Vicaire, Georges. Manuel de l'amateur de livres du XIXe siècle, 1801-1893. Paris: A. Rouquette, 1894-1920. Reprints. Teaneck [N.J.]: Somerset House, 1973. New York: B. Franklin, 1973.

Vindel, F. Arte tipográfico

Vindel, Francisco. El arte tipográfico en España durante el siglo XV. Madrid: Ministerio de Asuntos Exteriores, Relaciones Culturales, 1945-51.
----- El arte tipográfico en Cataluña durante el siglo XV: apéndice. Madrid: Dirección General de Relaciones Culturales, 1954.

Vindel, F. Manual

Vindel, Francisco. Manual gráfico-descriptivo del bibliófilo hispano-americano (1475-1850). Madrid, etc., 1930-31.
----- ----- Suplemento. 1934-

Wagner, H.R. Bib. mexicana

Wagner, Henry Raup. Nueva bibliografía mexicana del siglo XVI, suplemento a las bibliografías de don Joaquín García Icazbalceta, don José Toribio Medina y don Nicolás Léon. México: Editorial Polis, 1940 [i.e. 1946]

Wagner, H.R. Spanish Southwest

Wagner, Henry Raup. The Spanish Southwest, 1542-1794: an annotated bibliography. Albuquerque: The Quivira Society, 1937. Reprint. New York: Arno Press, 1967.

Wagner-Camp

Wagner, Henry Raup. The Plains and the Rockies: a bibliography of original narratives of travel and adventure, 1800-1865. Rev. by Charles I. Camp. 3rd ed. Columbus, Ohio: Long's College Book Co., 1953.

Ward, W.S. Index of serials

Ward, William Smith. Index and finding list of serials published in the British Isles, 1789-1832. Lexington: University of Kentucky Press, 1953.

Wegelin, O. Amer. poetry

Wegelin, Oscar. Early American poetry: a compilation of the titles and volumes of verse and broadsides by writers born or residing in North America, north of the Mexican border. New York: P. Smith, 1930.

Welch, D.A. Amer. children's books

Welch, D'Alte Aldridge. A bibliography of American children's books printed prior to 1821. Worcester, Mass.: American Antiquarian Society, 1972.

Wellcome cat. of printed books

Wellcome Historical Medical Library, London. <u>A catalogue of printed books in the Wellcome Historical Medical Library.</u> London: Wellcome Historical Medical Library, 1962-

Weller, E.O. Falsche Druckorte

Weller, Emil Ottokar. <u>Die falschen und fingierten Druckorte: Repertorium der seit Erfindung der Buchdruckerkunst unter falscher Firma erschienenen deutschen, lateinischen und französischen Schriften.</u> Hildesheim: G. Olms, 1960.
----- <u>Nachträge.</u> 1961.

Wheeler gift

American Institute of Electrical Engineers. Library. <u>Catalogue of the Wheeler gift of books, pamphlets, and periodicals in the library of the American Institute of Electrical Engineers.</u> Ed. by William D. Weaver. New York: American Institute of Electrical Engineers, 1909.

White, G. Engl. illustration

White, Gleeson. <u>English illustration, 'The sixties': 1855-70.</u> Westminster: A. Constable, 1897. Reprint. Bath: Kingsmead Reprints, 1970.

Wiener, J.H. Unstamped Brit. periodicals

Wiener, Joel H. <u>A descriptive finding list of unstamped British periodicals, 1830-1836.</u> London: Bibliographical Society, 1970.

Wierzbowski, T. Bib. Polonica

Wierzbowski, Teodor. <u>Bibliographia Polonica XV ac XVI ss.</u> Varsoviae: C. Kowalewsky, 1889-94.

Wiles, R.M. Freshest advices

Wiles, Roy McKeen. <u>Freshest advices: early provincial newspapers in England.</u> Columbus: Ohio State University Press, 1965.

Williams, I.A. 18th cent. bib.

Williams, Iolo Aneurin. <u>Seven XVIIIth century bibliographies.</u> London: Dulau, 1924. Reprint. New York: B. Franklin, 1968.

Winans, R.B. Book cats.

Winans, Robert B. A descriptive checklist of book catalogues separately printed in America, 1693-1800. Worcester: American Antiquarian Society, 1981.

Wing

Wing, Donald Goddard. Short-title catalogue of books printed in England, Scotland, Ireland, Wales, and British America, and of English books printed in other countries, 1641-1700. New York: Index Society, 1945-51.

Wing (2nd ed.)

Wing, Donald Goddard. Short-title catalogue of books printed in England, Scotland, Ireland, Wales, and British America, and of English books printed in other countries, 1641-1700. 2nd ed., rev. and enl. New York: Index Committee of the Modern Language Association of America, 1972-

Wing Foundation

Newberry Library, Chicago. John M. Wing Foundation. Dictionary catalogue of the history of printing from the John M. Wing Foundation in the Newberry Library. Boston: G.K. Hall, 1961.
----- First supplement. 1970.

Wisconsin. Chemical books

Wisconsin. University. Library. Chemical, medical, and pharmaceutical books printed before 1800, in the collections of the University of Wisconsin Libraries. Ed. by John Neu. Comp. by Samuel Ives, Reese Jenkins, and John Neu. Madison: University of Wisconsin Press, 1965.

Wise, T.J. Ashley lib.

Wise, Thomas James. The Ashley library, a catalogue of printed books, manuscripts, and autograph letters, collected by Thomas James Wise. London: Printed for private circulation only, 1922-36. Reprint. Folkestone: Dawsons of Pall Mall, 1971.

Wolfe, R.J. Secular music

Wolfe, Richard J. Secular music in America, 1801-1825: a bibliography. New York: The New York Public Library, 1964.

Wolff, R.L. 19th cent. fiction

Wolff, Robert Lee. Nineteenth-century fiction: a bibliographical catalogue based on the collection formed by Robert Lee Wolff. New York: Garland Pub., 1981-

Wood, C. Vertebrate zoology

Wood, Casey Albert. An introduction to the literature of vertebrate zoology: based chiefly on the titles in the Blacker Library of Zoology, the Emma Shearer Wood Library of ornithology, the Bibliotheca Osleriana and other libraries of the McGill University, Montreal. London: Oxford University Press, 1931. Reprint. New York: Arno Press, 1974.

Wright, L.H. Amer. fiction, 1774-1850 (2nd ed.)

Wright, Lyle Henry. American fiction, 1774-1850: a contribution toward a bibliography. 2nd rev. ed. San Marino, Calif.: Huntington Library, 1969.

Wright, L.H. Amer. fiction, 1851-1875

Wright, Lyle Henry. American fiction, 1851-1875: a contribution toward a bibliography. San Marino, Calif.: Huntington Library, 1965.

Wright, L.H. Amer. fiction, 1876-1900

Wright, Lyle Henry. American fiction, 1876-1900: a contribution toward a bibliography. San Marino, Calif.: Huntington Library, 1966.

Yale. Alchemy

Yale University. Library. Beinecke Rare Book and Manuscript Library. Alchemy and the occult: a catalogue of books and manuscripts from the collection of Paul and Mary Mellon given to Yale University Library. New Haven: Yale University Library, 1968-77.

Yale. Ornithological books

Yale University. Library. Ornithological books in the Yale University Library, including the library of William Robertson Coe. Comp. by S. Dillon Ripley and Lynette L. Scribner. New Haven: Yale University Press, 1961.

Zimmer, J.T. Ayer Lib.

Field Museum of Natural History, Chicago. Edward E. Ayer Ornithological Library. Catalogue of the Edward E. Ayer Ornithological Library. By John Todd Zimmer. Chicago: The Museum, 1926. Reprint. New York: Arno Press, 1974.

GPO 892-459